Water Quality Vital Signs Monitoring Protocol for the Pacific Island Network - Appendixes

Version 1.0

Natural Resource Report NPS/PACN/NRR—2011/419

Tahzay Jones, Danielle McKay, Kimber DeVerse, Kelly Kozar

National Park Service
Pacific Island Inventory and Monitoring Network
Hawaii Volcanoes National Park
PO Box 52
Hawaii National Park, Hawaii 96718

June 2011

U.S. Department of the Interior
National Park Service
Natural Resource Stewardship and Science
Fort Collins, Colorado

The National Park Service, Natural Resource Stewardship and Science office in Fort Collins, Colorado publishes a range of reports that address natural resource topics of interest and applicability to a broad audience in the National Park Service and others in natural resource management, including scientists, conservation and environmental constituencies, and the public.

The Natural Resource Report Series is used to disseminate high-priority, current natural resource management information with managerial application. The series targets a general, diverse audience, and may contain NPS policy considerations or address sensitive issues of management applicability.

All manuscripts in the series receive the appropriate level of peer review to ensure that the information is scientifically credible, technically accurate, appropriately written for the intended audience, and designed and published in a professional manner. This report received formal, high-level peer review based on the importance of its content, or its potentially controversial or precedent-setting nature. Peer review was conducted by highly qualified individuals with subject area technical expertise and was overseen by a peer review manager.

Views, statements, findings, conclusions, recommendations, and data in this report do not necessarily reflect views and policies of the National Park Service, U.S. Department of the Interior. Mention of trade names or commercial products does not constitute endorsement or recommendation for use by the U.S. Government.

This report is available from the Pacific Island I&M Network website (http://www.nature.nps.gov/im/units/pacn) and the Natural Resource Publications Management website (http://www.nature.nps.gov/publications/nrpm/).

Please cite this publication as:

NPS 988/108133, June 2011

Contents

Appendix A. Park Background Information for Current Strategic Plans

AMME: American Memorial Park

"On August 18, 1978 (P.L. 95-348), the U.S. Congress authorized and directed the U.S. National Park Service '...to develop, maintain and administer the existing American Memorial Park (AMME) located at Tanapag Harbor Reservation, Saipan. The park shall be administered for the primary purpose of honoring the dead in the World War II Mariana Island campaign.'"

The National Park Service was further directed to provide interpretation that describes the World War II battle for Saipan and its relationship to the World War II Marianas Campaign as a whole. Secondary interpretive themes would encompass the ecological and environmental resources of the park. Lastly, the early history of Saipan could be interpreted to explain its relationship to subsequent historical events.

American Memorial Park honors the American and Marianas people who died in the World War II Marianas Campaign. As a "living memorial" the park also creates a venue for community recreational, cultural and historical activities. The Court of Honor memorializes the Americans who died during the Marianas Campaign. The Marianas Memorial honors the Chamorro and Carolinian war dead.

In the early years of World War II, Japanese bunkers, pillboxes, antiaircraft gun emplacements, ammunition embrasures, a hospital, and other military quarters were developed within what is now the park boundary. The park contains Micro Beach, one of the islands finest white sand beaches. The park also contains the site of the landing of the first major Carolinian migration to Saipan. The beach within AMME was used by ancient Chamorro as a training beach for celestial navigators. Several areas within the park have cultural significance to the local Carolinian populations and are used for traditional ceremonies.

The .25-acre inland mangrove-wetland complex is unique to Saipan and has been designated as an "Area of Particular Concern" by the CNMI. The wetlands are a know habitat for the endangered nightingale reed warbler and the common moorhen.

WAPA: War in the Pacific National Historic Park

On August 18th, 1978 War in the Pacific National Historical Park was authorized by Public Law 95-348. The park is located on the Island of Guam. Guam lies 3,800 miles west of Hawaii and 1,600 miles east of the Philippines. It is the largest and southernmost island of the 15 Mariana Islands. The island is a US Flag Territory, and is the natural focus of activity within the Marianas and Micronesia. It is the largest and most populated island between Hawaii and the Philippines having an excellent well equipped port and is a major communications center.

This unique National Park honors the bravery and sacrifices of all those who participated in the Pacific Theater of World War II. This includes the United States, Japan, and the Allied nations; Australia, Canada, China, France, Great Britain, New Zealand, the Netherlands, and the Soviet Union. Park visitors have the opportunity to learn about the events that lead to the outbreak of the Pacific War, the Battle of Guam and the role the Mariana Islands played in helping to end World War II (1941-1945).

War in the Pacific National Historical Park (NHP) is comprised of 959 terrestrial acres and 1,002 marine acres. The resources of the park include invasion beaches and other sites important to the 1944 invasion and recapture of Guam during WWII, and as a result, each of the seven units contains some significant historic resources, including six that are listed on the National Register of Historic Places.

Approximately 1,000 acres (over half of total park area) of marine environment is equally divided between two ocean units (Asan Beach and Agat Beach units). These coral reefs contain significant marine resources, including two federally listed species of sea turtles. In addition to the WWII sites, there are sites of cultural importance for Guam's Chamorro population, many of these having marine-related significance. Four units (Agat Inland, Mt. Alifan units, Mt. Tenjo, and Fonte Plateau) contain 1,000 acres of tropical savanna, savanna vegetation recovering from fire, limestone and riverine forests with several streams and both coastal and inland wetlands. The remaining park unit, Piti Guns, is the site of an experimental forest and contains mahogany trees planted in the 1920s. The Asan Inland and beach units comprise an entire sub-watershed.

Mission of National Park Service at War in the Pacific NHP
The mission of the National Park Service at War in the Pacific NHP is rooted in and grows from the park's legislated mandate found in the Act of Congress. War in the Pacific National Historical Park (WAPA) was established (P.L. 95-348, section 6a) in 1978 "to commemorate the bravery and sacrifice of those participating in the campaigns of the Pacific theater of World War II [not only the United States and Japan, but includes Australia, Canada, China, France, Great Britain, the Netherlands, New Zealand, and the Soviet Union] and to conserve and interpret outstanding natural, scenic, and historic values and objects on the island of Guam for the benefit and enjoyment of present and future generations…" Included in WAPA's enabling mandate: other points on the island of Guam relevant to the park may be identified, established, and marked; interpretative activities will be conducted in the following three languages: English, Chamorro, and Japanese; and, the park may pursue berthing and interpretation of a naval vessel of World War II (WWII) vintage which shall be accessible to the public on the island of Guam. To the maximum extent feasible, the park is directed to employ and train residents of Guam or of the Northern Mariana Islands to develop, maintain, and administer the park; and, no fee or charge shall be imposed for entrance or admission.

Significance
War in the Pacific NHP the only site in the National Park System (comprised of 390 parks) that honors the bravery and sacrifices of all those who participated in the Pacific Theater of World War II. WAPA's museum collection contains approximately 10,000 artifacts and historic photographs related to the Pacific Theater of World War II.

The park contains sites important to the 1944 invasion and recapture of Guam during WWII, and as a result, each unit contains some significant resources. The following are included on the National Register of Historic Places: Agat and Asan Invasion Beaches, Asan Ridge Battle Park, Hill 40, Matgue River Valley Battlefield, Memorial Beach Park, and Piti Coastal Defense Guns. In addition to cultural resources significant to WWII, there are sites of cultural importance to the island's Chamorro resident population with many of these having marine-related importance. Over 3,500 marine species and 200 species of coral are located within the scuba and snorkeling areas of park waters.

Key External Factors Affecting Plan's Accomplishment

While park management and staff can plan, manage, and largely control much of what occurs in the park, other things they can only influence, especially things external to park boundaries. Some things, such as natural events, they have no control over whatsoever. In developing War in the Pacific NHP's Strategic Plan and its long-term goals, it was important to take into consideration key external factors that could negatively or positively affect goal outcomes. A few of the most important or most likely are identified briefly below. This is by no means an exhaustive list but simply those that are most likely to influence outcomes as viewed at the time of writing the plan.

Guam is an organized, unincorporated territory of the US with policy relations between Guam and the US under the jurisdiction of the US Department of the Interior, Office of Insular Affairs. The island's population is culturally diverse; in addition to the local Chamorro population, immigrants from mainland Asia, Japan, the Philippines, and nearly all of the islands of the Federated States of Micronesia have settled in Guam since WWII. With an estimated population of approximately 160,000 people, the economy is dependent primarily upon tourism.

Invasive and Alien Species

The only documented large invasive mammals in WAPA are *Cervus mariannus* (Philippine deer), feral pigs, feral cats, and feral dogs. To date there have been no studies examining their densities and impacts. Other invasive animals that have been observed in the park include *Bufo marianas* (marine toad), *Achatina fulica* (Giant African slug), *Carlia fusca* (curious skink), and *Boiga irregularis* (brown tree snake).

Many native birds have become extinct or endangered because of the brown tree snake (*Bolga irregularis*). Of War in the Pacific NHP's native forest birds, only the Guam swiftlet (*Aerodramus bartschi*) may be extant, the remainders are believed to be extinct. At the height of its invasion, *B. irregularis* numbered 12,000 snakes per square mile.

One of the most invasive plant species is *Leucaena leucocephala*, which was introduced to prevent erosion after the events of World War II. It has spread extensively, particularly on limestone soil. Another alien plant and potential threat is the mission grass that prevents re-establishment of the native savanna vegetation.

Fishing

Approximately one third of the submerged lands within WAPA are owned by the NPS; the remaining lands are owned by the Territory of Guam, which, through an MOU with NPS relinquished administrative control of these lands to WAPA. A condition of the MOU guarantees the continuation of traditional subsistence fishing within the park in accordance with territorial fishing regulations. The broad definition of "traditional" fishing used by the Government of Guam also adds further complexities. Proximity to large population centers and easy access have made the Agat and Asan marine units popular sites for fishing and recreation. The quantity of harvested fish and other marine life is poorly known. Observations made by park staff suggest the intensive fishing, which has been estimated at 30,000 fisherman-days per year, is having a noticeable effect on the nearshore environment. It is also suspected that commercial fisheries are occurring in the park waters. Knowledge of extraction rates would help to better manage fisheries within the park waters.

Adjacent Land Use

Adjacent land use, in the form of light industrial, commercial, and residential development encroaches on and poses a potential threat to park lands and waters. Guam has very poorly enforced zoning regulations. Human development comes to the very edge of the park boundary and, in some cases, has crossed onto park lands. Guam also does not have an approved Coastal Zone Management Plan, so regulations overseeing development along the coast are not complete. The primary north-south road on the island runs adjacent to park waters. Several buildings have been constructed along the coast, and many directly abut the ocean. Development in the watersheds above both the Asan and Agat Beach units is considerable and anti-erosion regulations are inconsistently enforced by local regulatory agencies during construction.

Erosion & Sedimentation

One of the greatest threats to the health and survival of Guam's coral reefs are sediment loads carried by streams and rivers. Sediment can harm coral reefs by either smothering them or by decreasing light availability needed for zooxanthellae (symbiont that sequester energy) to photosynthesize. Sedimentation accumulates on WAPA's coral reefs from several sources, relating primarily to poor land management practices. Those sources can include wildfires and urban development. Wildfires are intentional, resulting from human activities relating to agriculture, the facilitation of hunting pigs and deer, and arson. Fires do not occur naturally in high frequencies; therefore the native vegetation is not adapted to these rates of burning. After the fire, soil bare of anchoring vegetation is readily washed into rivers and streams and eventually to the nearshore environment. Within the park, up to 20% of the terrain is burned each year, constituting a major threat, stressor, and land management issue.

NPSA: National Park of American Samoa

The National Park of American Samoa (NPSA) was established in 1988 by PL 100-571 with park lands on the islands of Tutuila, Ofu and Ta'u in the Territory of American Samoa. The park's purpose is "to preserve and protect the tropical rainforest and archeological and cultural resources of American Samoa, and of associated reefs, to maintain the habitat of flying foxes, preserve the ecological balance of the Samoan tropical forest, and consistent with the preservation of these resources, to provide for the enjoyment of the unique resources of the Samoan tropical forest by visitors from around the world". Because the Park could not purchase land outright due to traditional communal land system, it was not until 1993 that the park became legally established with a 50-year lease agreement. The park consists of 7,970 acres of land and 2,550 marine acres (NPSA's boundary extends 0.25 miles offshore where water depths are about 100 ft).

NPSA's paleotropical rainforests and Indo-Pacific coral reefs are unique to the NPS system. The diversity of terrestrial species is low due to the isolation of the Samoan islands, but approximately 30% of the plants and one bird species are endemic to the archipelago. The only native mammal species are three species of bats. Other important terrestrial resources are birds,

4

reptiles, coconut crabs, and stream ecosystems. The marine system, in contrast, is highly diverse with some 900 fish and over 200 coral species, as well as rare and endangered sea turtles and humpback whales. Over 100 nearshore species are harvested for food.

A major terrestrial priority is the control of invasive species, particularly alien plants and feral pigs. In the marine environment, perhaps the major issue is lessening the impacts of climate change on coral reefs; we are already seeing an increased incidence of coral bleaching and disease that is associated with warmer water temperatures. A high priority for both terrestrial and marine programs is to develop monitoring programs to track changes through time.

USAR: USS Arizona Memorial

Legislation and Mission Statement
The USS Arizona Memorial was established by Public Law 85-344, March 15, 1958 which authorized construction and maintenance of the USS Arizona Memorial and museum. Public Law 87-201, September 6, 1961, authorized appropriations for the construction of the memorial. On March 21, 1980, the Navy authorized the National Park Service to operate the USS Arizona Memorial through a Use Agreement. It is located 7.5 miles from downtown Honolulu, Hawaii. Containing 11 acres, the park preserves and interprets the tangible historical resources associated with the December 7, 1941 Japanese attack on Pearl Harbor and other military installations on the island of Oahu. Of primary importance are the sunken hull of the USS Arizona, which serves as the final resting place for many of the battleship's sailors and marines killed in that attack, and the memorial structure which straddles the ship and is dedicated to all those US military that lost their lives on December 7, 1941. The park also interprets the historical events which led up to and which were a direct result of the December 7th attack. The park was also established to preserve and interpret the intangible historical values; the memories, attitudes, and traditions of those individuals who were present at or had intimate first-hand knowledge of the historic events which took place on December 7, 1941. This valuable part of America's heritage is made available to approximately 1.5 million international visitors each year for their experience, enlightenment, understanding, and appreciation.

Significance
The resources at the USS Arizona Memorial are nationally significant for many reasons. It provides a venue for the National Park Service to honor and commemorate the American servicemen and civilians who lost their lives during the December 7, 1941 attack. The Pearl Harbor attack acted as a catalyst to bring the United States fully and actively into World War II and as a rallying cry to unify the country in that case. This attack is one of the most well remembered and significant events in the history of our nation.

Many military sites on the island of Oahu were attacked; 2,390 Americans were killed as a result of the attack; over 320 aircraft were destroyed or damaged and 21 vessels were sunk or damaged. The USS Arizona represents the greatest loss of life on a military vessel in American Naval history. The sunken hull of the USS Arizona remains in place and its 1,177 casualties accounted for almost half of all the casualties sustained that day. The sunken battleship became a tomb and therefore a symbol of commemoration and place of remembrance for the December 7, 1941 attack. The salvage of the Pacific Fleet at Pearl Harbor is considered the greatest maritime salvage operation in history. The events of December 7, 1941 and its aftermath profoundly affected the people of Hawaii and those throughout the nation.

Organization

The USS Arizona Memorial staff is lead by a superintendent. Staff is organized into three operating teams: 1) Law Enforcement, Interpretation and Resource Management, 2) Maintenance, and 3) Administration. It is a future goal to update the park organizational chart and divide these into five teams with each specialty identified answering directly to the superintendent or an assistant superintendent. Staff expertise and specialties on the Law Enforcement, Interpretation, Resource Management Team include 1 chief ranger, 1 deputy chief ranger, 7 permanent park rangers, 1 historian, 1 curator, 2 projectionists, 1 permanent park guide, and approximately 16 seasonal park guides (8 seasonals for six months and then another 8 seasonals for six months). It is the hope of park management to convert the seasonal guides to 8 permanent guides and bring on one additional seasonal in the summer. This would bring the park into compliance with regulations and save time and money in recruitment, hiring, training and would promote continuity. The Maintenance Team includes 1 facility manager, 1 work leader, 3 maintenance workers, 1 permanent custodian/grounds worker, 2 permanent custodians, and 2 or 3 seasonal custodians. The Administration Team is made up of 1 administrative officer, 1 human relations specialist/administrative technician, and 1 supply technician.

Our staff will be supplemented and assisted by various other National Park Service (NPS) sites and central offices, and/or other partners or organizations. The US Navy will be the contracting officer for the construction of a replacement visitor center and museum facility and a separate headquarters building. This will ensure we have satisfactory facilities to achieve appropriate goals. The Western Archaeological Conservation Center will continue to assist with our collections so we can make informed decisions about our artifacts. The Submerged Resources Center will assist with research and monitoring on the USS Arizona. The University of Hawaii is assisting in the partnership between NOAA and The NPS to manage a Japanese mini-submarine found off the coast of Pearl Harbor that was involved in the December 7, 1941 attack.

The Arizona Memorial Museum Association (AMMA) who operates and manages the bookstore will continue to provide valuable assistance for education, interpretation, and research. AMMA was requested by the NPS to raise funds for the replacement visitor center and museum. As a result AMMA is in the process of a major, 34 million dollar, capital fundraising campaign.

Increasing visitation is always a desire but it is important not to do so at the expense of the visitor experience or the resource. It is the desire of park management to institute a partial reservation system. This would enhance the visitor experience for those that wanted to take advantage of it. Currently the program tickets are first come first serve so the park gets inundated with visitors in the morning and tickets can be gone by 11:00 AM. The last program is at 3:00 PM so that means people may have to wait up to four hours. It is not uncommon to have 20 to 30 empty seats for a program because visitors elected not to return. A reservation system would improve this and other situations and hopefully can be implemented in the future. The park has been told not to move forward with a reservation system of any kind until a law suite that affects reservations nationwide has been settled.

Another way to increase visitation would be to extend the hours of operation. This would take a very large base increase so this is a vision for the future and, although considered, beyond the scope of this plan.

Community Relations
It is vital to have quality relationships with the community. The Navy works with us on a variety of issues, from special events, security, construction projects, to building new shuttle boats. The Navy has state and federal money (about twelve million dollars) to replace the visitor shuttle boats and has brought us in for consultation and as a stakeholder. Some of our non-profit neighbors include the USS Bowfin Submarine Museum and Park, the USS Missouri, and the Pearl Harbor Historic Trail. The trail has minimal visitation but does start within the park and would like to increase their visitation.

A new neighbor is Ford Island Ventures (FIV) which has leased the property between the Bowfin and the USS Arizona Memorial from the Navy for 65 years. FIV is a for profit company that through its lease with the Navy is permitted to operate commercial ventures. The concern is that FIV will put one or more of the non-profits out of business. Many consider this area sacred and feel it should not be commercialized. FIV says they will maintain a 1942 theme, have people answer questions about all the sites in the area, and will bring more business to the Bowfin and Missouri, not take it away. The result remains to be seen because FIV has not completed their development.

Facilities
Park facilities that help accomplish our goals include: 1 visitor center with exhibits, 2 theaters, 1 museum, 1 maintenance building, a small concession operation, support offices and the memorial. The capital campaign mentioned, and the decision to replace the visitor center was not made lightly. The NPS had two separate engineering companies evaluate the structural integrity of the building. Both firms determined independently that even with modifications the existing visitor center had a life expectancy of three to eight years from now (2008–2012). In addition, the current visitor center and museum was designed to accommodate about 750,000 visitors a year while on average we receive 1.5 million per year. The inadequacies of the bathroom facilities alone warrant new restrooms not to mention the additional problems with poor pedestrian traffic flow and circulation through the visitor center and its exhibits.

In the past the park, USS Arizona Memorial, listed seven structures on their List of Classified Structures. In the five year plan that number has been adjusted to reflect the structures that are included within our use agreement and land assignment with the Navy. Those are: the USS Arizona, the memorial above her, and the Circle of Remembrance exhibit. In the future we will pursue a memorandum of understanding with the Navy about the USS Utah and its mooring quays, plaques, and any other artifacts that we feel are appropriate.

It is the hope of the superintendent to acquire six bungalows on Ford Island from the Navy. These were noncommissioned officer's homes built in the 1920s and 1930s and are the last homes like this in the area. Sailors and Marines sought protection in these building during the attack. In addition, saving these structures would protect the view shed and soundscape from the memorial. They would be used for offices, storage of artifacts, and a dive locker which is desperately needed. The Navy wants the NPS to have these structures and is currently in negotiations to lease them to us at no cost. The homes need a lot of work but cultural specialists believe they are well worth saving. A hazardous analysis of the bungalows was done and upon the completion of that the regional office has been supportive of the park acquiring those buildings.

Resource Assessment
The resource assessment establishes the availability of human and fiscal resources, the condition of the park's natural, cultural, and recreational resources and the condition of the visitor experience. The assessment of resources assists the park in developing realistic and meaningful long term goals and helps identify potential organizational improvements.

Natural Resources
The USS Arizona is home to a large collection of vertebrate and invertebrate natural resources. The natural process of biofouling has significantly contributed to the preservation of the ship. This biofouling has provided the basis for the ship's transformation into an artificial reef. Perhaps most notable of the ship's natural resources are the threatened green turtles, many of which make the ship their home. As such, the management of the natural resources plays an important role in both the natural and cultural preservation of the park.

Cultural Resources
The USS Arizona Memorial is one of the most important historical sites within the National Park Service both for the importance of the event it commemorates and its relevance to the outcome of WWII. The submerged USS Arizona is the most significant physical artifact of the Japanese attack on Oahu. Older visitors who may have lived through the era of World War II and younger visitors who have only read about the event come to the site to make the physical connection to this tragic day in American history. The recent nature of the attack has contributed to an unusual range of interpretive resources for the USS Arizona Memorial. The most significant of these resources are the actual survivors, many of whom volunteer at the park or add to its growing collection.

USS Arizona
The primary cultural resource of the park is the ship USS Arizona. Due to the submerged nature of the remaining hulk, the actual condition of the ship is difficult to determine. Approximately 90% of the exterior hull structure of the ship has been surveyed, while less than 5% of the interior spaces have been surveyed by Remote Operating Vehicle (ROV). The ship is a maritime grave and war tomb. It holds the remains of over 900 sailors and Marines whose bodies were never recovered. The Arizona is a resource of highest quality; its size and location have helped to ensure its preservation. The memorial structure above the ship (while over 40 years old), has acquired a considerable amount of historical significance and is recorded on the park's List of Classified Structures (LCS).

The memorial shrine wall lists the names of the 1,177 sailors and Marines who lost their lives as a result of the attack, in addition to the names of those survivors who have had their ashes interred on the ship since 1980.

List of Classified Structures

There were seven structures listed on the List of Classified Structures for the USS Arizona Memorial; the USS Arizona, the USS Arizona Memorial, the USS Arizona and Vestal Quays, the Pearl Harbor Naval Base Pearl Harbor NHL, the Remembrance Exhibit, the USS Utah, and the USS Utah Memorial. Three structures are actually within the land assignment and use agreement the National Park Service has with the Navy, the USS Arizona, the memorial above it, and the Remembrance Exhibit. The USS Arizona is listed in "unknown" condition. The Remembrance Exhibit is listed as "fair" condition due to corrosion on the topographic map display. The memorial is in "good" condition.

Museum Collection

Currently there are approximately 4,400 catalogued items in the museum collection with an additional 30,000 items (the 14th Naval District Photo Collection) presently being catalogued. Approximately 450 Pearl Harbor Survivor oral histories have been recorded, many on video tape. These oral histories contain a considerable amount of baseline information and are an irreplaceable resource.

Visitor Use Resources

In 2004, 1.574 million people visited the park. The interpretive program consists of a brief talk by a park guide or volunteer, followed by a 23 minute documentary film on the Pearl Harbor attack. Immediately after the film, the guide or volunteer escorts the visitors to the boat landing, where they board a Navy shuttle to the memorial located adjacent to Ford Island in Pearl Harbor. Visitors disembark on the memorial to view the ship and the shrine room for approximately 10 minutes, returning to the visitor center on the shuttle boat. The entire program lasts 1 hour and 15 minutes. Programs to the USS Arizona Memorial operate from 8:00 a.m. to 3:00 p.m. and are offered 362 days per year. The visitor center is open separate from the organized programs from 7:30 a.m. to 5:00 p.m. Information is disseminated from the front lobby desk area. A new 7 language audio tour is available for visitors before beginning the program that enables them to better understand what they are about to experience on the shuttle boat, at the memorial and back at the visitor center and museum. The audio program is available for $5, a portion of which is returned to fund educational programs at the park through the park cooperating association, the Arizona Memorial Museum Association (AMMA).

Prior to the formal program, visitors may explore the museum and browse through the bookstore operated by the AMMA. Other facilities in the visitor center include a small concession area, central courtyard, restrooms and administrative areas. The lawn behind the visitor center offers wayside exhibits explaining different aspects of the December 7th attack. The Remembrance Exhibit is also located on the back lawn and lists the names of those who lost their lives at locations other than the USS Arizona as a result of the attack on the island. Expansive lawn areas with shade trees are available for visitors waiting for their programs. The areas are used by families and tour groups for relaxation, picnicking, and quiet reflection.

Emergency Services and Visitor Protection

Since September 11, 2001, protection of the USS Arizona Memorial has changed. The memorial is considered a possible "soft" (non-military) target. The U.S. Navy has directed the NPS to institute significant security measures. In 2004, a deputy chief ranger was hired, this person is the senior law enforcement officer at the USS Arizona Memorial. He is in charge of law enforcement, physical security, emergency medical operations (EMS), anti-terrorism, safety, and the coordination of multiple agencies in achieving this mission. He also serves as the Contracting Technical Representative for a three guard security contingent. In 2004, one additional park ranger (protection) was hired. In FY-05, two more rangers will be hired. In addition to the permanent NPS employees hired, a security company was contracted to provide three security guards 10 hours daily. One of the guards works the check point to ensure that no bags are carried into the visitor center while two others patrol the parking lots on bikes. The security guards have been an effective deterrent to criminals who break into cars, which had been a huge problem. Emergency services are provided to visitors by Federal Fire stationed at Naval Station Pearl Harbor. Federal Fire can respond in less that five minutes and can provide full Advanced Life Support services and transportation to local hospitals.

Key External Factors Affecting Plan's Accomplishment

While park management and staff can plan, manage, and largely control much of what occurs in the park, other things they can only influence, especially things external to park boundaries. Some things, such as natural events, they have no control over whatsoever. In developing the USS Arizona Memorial's Strategic Plan and its long-term goals, it was important to take into consideration key external factors that could negatively or positively affect goal outcomes.

KALA: Kalaupapa National Historic Park

Kalaupapa National Historical Park's annual goals for FY 2005 will be accomplished using the organization, facilities, and financial resources summarized below. These should give the park staff, partners, stakeholders, and the public a better understanding of not only what we are trying to accomplish this year, but also how we are doing it in a very real sense.

Organization

Superintendent, Tom Workman, leads the Kalaupapa National Historical Park staff. The staff is organized into five operating divisions: Visitor Protection, Natural Resource Management, Cultural Resource Management, Maintenance and Historic Preservation, and Administration. Staff expertise and specialties include two permanent Law Enforcement park rangers, under the Visitor Protection program who are responsible for the management and training of the NPS Fire Department, emergency medical services, and law enforcement.

The Natural and Cultural Resource Management programs each have a Division Chief. The Natural Resource Division has a Marine Ecologist working on coral reef issues and is assisted by an employee of the Cooperative Ecosystems Studies Unit. The Natural Resource Management program will gain one additional coral reef management staff member to act as a Boat/Diver logistics person. The Cultural Resource Division has a curator position available. The Division is assisted by Cooperative Ecosystems Studies Unit employees.

The Maintenance and Historic Preservation Divisions have the bulk of park employees. The Maintenance Division has a WS supervisor, a high voltage electrician, a water system operator/repairer, 4 maintenance workers and the Historic Preservation Division has one Lead Exhibit Specialist and 3 carpenters. The park's administrative functions are conducted by the Administrative Officer and a Maintenance Clerk.

Our staff will be supplemented and/or supported this year using special project funds, contracts, and the assistance or expertise of various other NPS parks and central offices, and/or other partners or organizations, such as Student Conservation Assistants and Volunteers-in-Parks. They will assist other divisions in accomplishing their goals. NPS assistance in achieving specific park FY2008 annual goals will be provided by the National Park Service's Pacific Islands Support Office. The University of Hawaii and the State of Hawaii Department of Health will provide additional, vital assistance through cooperative agreement services or contracts. In addition to helping accomplish education and visitor services, Arizona Memorial Museum Association will provide sales clerks at the bookstore at no cost to NPS. Moloka'i Mule Rides contribute significantly to achieving our public service goals as well as assisting with the rehabilitation and maintenance of the historic Pali Trail.

Facilities

Park facilities and infrastructure for accomplishing the FY2008 annual goals includes: beaches, 3.3 miles of hiking trails, 12 miles of roadways, central maintenance facility, main park headquarters, 18 employee housing units for on-site protection and management of park resources, two dormitories for VIP and seasonal housing. There are over 200 Historic structures, one lighthouse, and several cemeteries with about 2,300 grave sites.

Financial Resources

Financial resources available to achieve the park's FY2008 annual goals include a base operating budget of approximately $2,500,000, which funds a permanent work force of 22 permanent positions, and 5 term positions. This work force will be supplemented by approximately 3,000 hours of Volunteers-in-Parks service, one Student Conservation Assistant, and special project and program funds distributed by the National Park Service regional and Washington offices. The park has cooperative agreements with the University of Hawaii to provide staff for the Natural and Cultural Resource programs. Achieving our FY2008 annual goal performance targets is critically dependent on our base funding and on these additional project funds, volunteer assistance, partnerships, and donations. We need to propose annual goals and organize the year's work in order to accomplish them as well as communicate and document all objectives and achievements. Therefore, all funding and staffing sources and major alternative sources of support and work, are included in the development of our Annual Performance Plan.

HALE : Haleakala National Park

Haleakala National Park is a vital part of America's national system of parks, monuments, battlefields, recreation areas, and other natural and cultural resources. Established by act of the United States Congress in August 1916 as the Haleakala section of Hawaii National Park, Haleakala became a separate unit on September 1960. The park is located on the island of Maui and contains over 30,000 acres. The park preserves Haleakala volcano and native Hawaiian ecosystems in perpetuity and makes this valuable part of America's heritage available to over 1.7 million visitors each year for their experience, enjoyment, understanding, and appreciation.

The park extends from sea level to the 10,023 ft. elevation. There are two areas of operations: Kïpahulu and the Summit, which is the location of the administrative headquarters. Each area has unique natural and cultural resources. Neither is managed as an autonomous unit. Management is a shared responsibility among park program managers.

Public Law 94-567 designated 19,720 acres of wilderness in the park under the Wilderness Act of 1964 with an additional 5,500 acres as Potential Wilderness. Currently, the park has 24,719 designated wilderness acres. In 1980 United Nations Education Scientific and Cultural Organization designated Haleakala National Park as an International Biosphere Reserve. Thirty-six of the park's species of plants, birds and insects are threatened or endangered and come under the protection of the Endangered Species Act of 1973.

In 1991, the park signed a Memorandum of Understanding as a partner in the East Maui Watershed Partnership whose purpose is to protect watershed resources and native ecosystems. Partners include the National Park Service, Hawai'i Department of Land and Natural Resources, County of Maui, The Nature Conservancy, East Maui Irrigation Company, Haleakala Ranch and Hana Ranch. In 1995, the park signed a cooperative agreement with Kïpahulu 'Ohana, Inc. to assist the park in protecting and interpreting Hawaiian culture.

Impact to native Hawaiian biota from alien species continues to be a major threat. The park had been actively promoting improved quarantine and inspection programs at Kahului Airport to prevent the establishment of invasive alien species. The park's efforts have come to fruition as the new quarantine facilities are currently under construction at Kahului Airport.

Visitor congestion in the morning at the summit and increasing numbers of commercial services have been ongoing problems. The situation is being addressed and the park is currently in the process of producing a Commercial Services Plan/environmental assessment. The Plan should be completed by FY 2008.

Mission Statements
Haleakala National Park is dedicated to preserving a nationally significant portion of Haleakala Volcano and unique native Hawaiian ecosystems. It allows public access to many of its geologic, scientific, scenic, and historic features. It also offers opportunities for recreation, education, inspiration, and enjoyment. The mission statement of the National Park Service at Haleakala National Park grows from the park's congressionally legislated mandate found in An Act to Establish a National Park in the Territory of Hawai'i, approved August 1, 1916 (39 Stat. 432) and supplemented by the National Park Service Organic act of August 1916. Our mission statement is a synthesis of our mandated purpose and the park's primary significance.

Purpose Statements
The purpose of Haleakala National Park is to preserve unique native Hawaiian ecosystems, scenic character, and associated Hawaiian culture. It also intends to provide educational, inspirational, and recreational opportunities compatible with preserving natural and cultural resources values.

Significance Statements
Haleakala National Park represents highly diverse volcanic, geological, and biological habitat ranging from over 10,000 feet elevation (highest point on Maui, third highest in the state) to sea level. It contains one of the few relatively intact remnants of a unique and disappearing Hawaiian biota found no other place in the world and designated as part of the biosphere reserve system. It includes the remote, pristine Haleakalä wilderness acclaimed for its attributes of beauty, serenity

and tranquility and where visitors can temporarily retreat from civilized society. It is an important component in East Maui Watershed Partnership whose preservation is the objective of a multiorganizational effort. Additionally, it has Class I air quality designation.

The park also contains abundant archeological and historical remains of the pre-European contact Hawaiian civilization. It is of religious and cultural importance to the Native Hawaiian community. It has many historical and cultural sites listed on the National Register of Historic Places.

Haleakala is also significant due to the opportunities it offers visitors and residents alike. It is Maui's number one tourist destination and, therefore, an integral part of the tourist-based economy of the island. It also provides outdoor recreational and educational opportunities unavailable elsewhere on Maui to the public.

Accomplishing Goals

Haleakala National Park staff is led by a Superintendent who is assisted by a Management Assistant. Staff is organized into five divisions: Protection, Interpretation, Resource Management, Maintenance, and Administration. There are two areas of operations: the Summit which includes Haleakala Crater and Kïpahulu which includes Kipahulu, Puhilele, Ka`apahu and Kaupo areas.

Staff expertise and specialties can be summarized by division. The Protection and Fee Division includes the Chief Ranger, an Operations Supervisory Ranger, 5 Park Rangers, 7 Visitor Use Assistants (2 Term), Commercial and Visitor Use Specialist, Supervisory Visitor Use Assistant, Lead Visitor Use Assistant and a Fee Program Clerk.

Interpretation Division includes the Chief of Interpretation, 4 Park Ranger Interpreters, 3 Park Guides, and an Administrative Support Clerk. Resources Management Division, under base funding, includes a Chief of Resources Management, shared clerk with Maintenance, Cultural Resource Program Manager and Archeologist, Natural Resources Program Manager for Vegetation Management, Wildlife Biologist Program Manager, Botanist, Entomologist, Wildlife Biologist as well as 4 Resource Park Rangers, and 7 Biological Science Technicians. There are 9 term employees with one base-funded Biological Technician and 8 non-base staff with 6 Biological Science Technicians, a Laborer, and a Museum Technician.

Administration Division includes the Superintendent, Management Assistant, Administrative Officer, Budget Analyst, Purchasing Agent, and an Administrative Systems Technician. Maintenance includes the Chief of Maintenance/Facility Manager, shared Maintenance Clerk with Resources Management, Maintenance Clerk (Temp), Maintenance Mechanic Supervisor, Maintenance Mechanic, 2 Waste Water Treatment Operators, 6 Maintenance Workers (3 Term), Volunteer Program Coordinator (Term), Facility Management Specialist (Term), an Electrician (Term), Trail Maintenance Worker Leader (Term), Animal Caretaker (Term), 3 Laborers (Seasonal), 3 Motor Vehicle Operators, 1 Facility Management Systems Coordinator (Intermittent) and a Maintenance Worker Helper.

Our staff will be supplemented and/or supported by assistance or expertise from various other NPS central offices, and/or other partners or organizations. These include the National Park

Service's Pacific West Regional Offices in Honolulu, Oakland, and Seattle as well as the Denver Service Center and Harpers Ferry Center in West Virginia.

The Hawai'i Natural History Association, helps accomplish education and visitor service goals through literature sales, providing sales clerks at visitor centers, and assisting with interpretive visitor services at no direct cost to the Federal Government. Friends of Haleakalä National Park, Inc. assists with a variety of service projects and raises funds for park programs and endangered species management. The United States Geological Survey-Biological Resources Division Scientist and staff maintains a presence in the park. They provide significant research assistance focused on park related problems funded by their agency.

Facilities

Park facilities utilized for accomplishing FY 2007-2011 annual goals includes: 1 visitor centers with exhibits and interpretive literature sales, 2 combination visitor center and central office buildings, 5 office buildings, 1 laundry facility, 15 wayside exhibits, 4 campgrounds, 13.88 miles of paved roads, 45.75 miles of trails, 3 trail bridges, 1 road bridge, 8 parking areas, 47.3 miles of fence, 2 picnic areas, 18 pit/chemical/vault toilets, 7 sewage systems, 5 backcountry visitor/employee cabins, 1 radio system, 1 computer network, 10 employee quarters, 1 garage, 1 summit overlook shelter, 2 crater rim overlook shelters, 1 picnic shelter, 1 gasoline station, 1 entrance station, 2 hazardous material storage sheds, 3 Yurts, 1 carpenter shop, 1 photovoltaic water pump and treatment system, 16 water storage tanks and 11 storage warehouse/sheds. Additionally, the park has many printed handouts and literature specific to HALE.

Program Evaluations

Haleakala National Park in 1996 was selected as a pilot park for developing the first GPRA plan in the Pacific Island Cluster of parks in the Pacific West Region. Park staff used the prescribed 8-step process to arrive at our mission statement, mission goals, and long-term goals. Annual accountability reviews have provided adjustment of budget and personnel to accomplish GPRA annual goals. Park program managers are annually evaluated on their responsiveness and success in reaching GPRA goals for which they share responsibility. When annual goals were not fully achieved, an analysis was done to examine why including whether or not the target was realistic. Visitor surveys have been instrumental in understanding the level of satisfaction, appreciation, and education visitors to the park enjoy. The breakdown of programs and facility ratings are invaluable in pinpointing where improvement needs to be focused. As of 2007, new goals and an update of this plan are required as the Department of Interior has established or deleted new goals service-wide as well as department-wide.

Key External Factors

External factors for FY 2007 that may negatively affect goal accomplishment include the following:

The introduction of a new alien species. Should a new alien plant or animal become established that would adversely affect park ecosystems, funds may be diverted to take immediate actions to deal with the problem.

The addition of new lands, including the Nu`u parcel, will stretch the current staffing as additional archeological surveys, more feral animal fencing in conjunction with feral animal removal, and more alien plant control and native plant restoration projects are needed to begin management of the area. No additional funding will come with the new acreages.

Park management and staff can plan, manage, and control much of what occurs in the park. Sometimes they can influence factors external to park boundaries that affect the park. Other factors, such as natural events, are beyond managing or influencing. All of these things can negatively or positively affect goal outcomes. A few of the most important or most likely to induce change are briefly identified below. This is not an exhaustive list but simply those factors that are most likely to influence outcomes at the time this plan was written.

The popularity of Haleakala National Park is expected to continue and presents even greater challenges both in terms of cultural and natural resource preservation and visitor use. The continued growth of the tourist industry and the high number of international visitors has placed special demands on park staff. Many factors will affect performance of this park. The cost of maintaining and restoring natural and cultural resources is escalating. It is difficult to improve the status of 36 threatened or endangered species in the park due to past loss of habitat and competition from alien species. The park will need to implement new programs that emphasize wise use of limited resources and sustainable practices. A significant increase in the number of projects requiring compliance reviews under the National Environmental Policy Act and/or Section 106 of the Historic Preservation Act. The National Parks and Omnibus Act of 1998 (Public Law 105-391) established major new responsibilities for concessions management, employee training and career development, natural resources inventory and monitoring, and cooperative research studies.

PUHE: Pu'ukohala Heiau National Historical Site
Pu'ukohola Heiau National Historic Site was established by an Act of Congress in 1972. It is located on the northwest coast of Hawaii Island. Containing about 80 acres, the park preserves historic stone built temples and associated sites in perpetuity and makes this valuable part of America's heritage available to over 200,000 visitors each year for their experience, enjoyment, understanding, and appreciation. The purpose of Pu'ukohola Heiau NHS is to restore and preserve the historically significant temple associated with Kamehameha the Great, the property of John Young, and the cultural landscape (circa AD 1790-1835).

Significance
The Pu`ukohola Heiau is a national historic landmark designated in 1962. It was designated as a historical landmark by the Department of Public Works, Territory of Hawai`i in 1928. These designations were made for many reasons that indicate its cultural significance to the Hawaiian people. A momentous, single event happened at this site, affecting all Hawaiian history to the present day. This is where Kamehameha I established his supremacy through the sacrifice of his chief rival, his cousin Keoua Kuahu'ula, on the temple altar and where he began his final successful effort to establish a Hawaiian kingdom. Pu'ukohola Heiau National Historic Site is closely associated with Kamehameha I and the unification of the Hawaiian Islands.

The location of Pu'ukohola Heiau was chosen regarding the visual alignment of the Kona coast and Maui, its elevated position on Pu'ukohola "Hill of the Whale", the fulfillment of prophecy, and the proximity of two other temples. The park contains examples of three types of heiau illustrating traditional Hawaiian religious practices: Pu`ukohola Heiau was a ceremonial luakini or state temple where human sacrifices were offered and dedicated to the war god Kuka`ilimoku; Mailekini Heiau was either luakini or an agricultural heiau, and the submerged Hale o Kapuni Heiau was dedicated to sharks, believed to be ancestral 'aumakua. Offshore waters contain one of the largest gatherings of black-tipped sharks in the State of Hawai`i. Many believe that Hale o Kapuni spiritually attracts sharks to the bay as in the years when the sharks were fed regularly at the submerged temple by the chief Alapa`ikupalupalumano.

Pelekane was a residence of Kamehameha I and several of his family, including wives and descendants who were also important figures in 19th century Hawai`i. The John Young property with its archeological site contains the first-known examples of western-style structures built in the islands; the property is also associated with western contact and influence through John Young's participation or witness to events important in the founding and early decades of the Hawaiian kingdom.

Key External Factors

While park management and staff can plan, manage, and largely control much of what occurs in the park, other things they can only influence, especially things external to park boundaries. Some things, such as natural events, they have no control over whatsoever. In developing Pu'ukohola Heiau NHS's Strategic Plan and its long term goals, it was important to take into consideration key external factors that could negatively or positively affect goal outcomes. A few of the most important or most likely to induce change are identified briefly below. This is by no means an exhaustive list but simply those that are most likely to influence outcomes as viewed at the time of writing the plan.

Visitor use patterns are strongly influenced by the Hawaiian tourism industry and are closely tied to each island's long-range economic development plans. These externally influenced use patterns strongly impact the ability of the park's staff and infrastructure to accommodate the visitors when they arrive. This issue involves not only increased visitation and its impact on park infrastructure and resources, but also other operational areas such as learning cultural behaviors and developing alternative means of communication for foreign visitors.

The economic base of the Island of Hawaii is in transition. New economic options are being pursued. The park must play a role in ensuring that any economic endeavor adjacent to the park does not become a threat to the park and its resources. In recent years, economic ventures proposed for adjacent land included a golf course and fairway homes, a 58-megawatt power plant, and development of the Hawaiian Homes Lands in Kawaihae. The jetties for a recreational boat harbor (90+/- slips) bordering the park's northern boundary were completed in FY97, though the construction of on shore facilities including a boat launching ramp, concessions, etc. are still pending with the State of Hawaii, Dept. of Transportation / Harbors Division. Further development by the State of Hawai'i Harbors Division to implement their 2020 plan to expand the commercial portion of the Kawaihae harbor still threatens their encroachment upon the park's proposed boundaries, in addition to implementing their upcoming plans with the Super Ferry providing inter-island transport and travel.

Native Hawaiians are seeking sovereignty. Various local groups are actively pursuing several forms of Hawaiian sovereignty. The National Park Service cannot escape involvement in this process since it preserves cultural and sacred sites that are necessary for the perpetuation of the traditional values of Native Hawaiian culture. A formal consultation process as well as the maintenance of informal resources in the Native Hawaiian community are essential for ensuring that the traditional needs of the Native Hawaiian community are met while at the same time ensuring the resources and the quality park experience are preserved and maintained.

State Highway 270 (Kawaihae Road) is currently the main road used to access the small fishing town of Kawaihae and North Kohala. This road bisects the park and presents a major hazard to visitors who attempt to visit the northern section of the park due to increased traffic on the road, particularly large trucks heading to or leaving the Kawaihae commercial harbor. The park is steadily working with the State of Hawaii/Dept. of Transportation–Highways Division on installing a bypass road and all other issues concerning the highway.

Commercial air tours and Military overflights adversely impact the visitor experience in the park, and potentially create vibrations that are detrimental to the mortarless stone temples. Local communications with both groups have been established and are maintained to help improve the visitor experience to the park and reduce potential threat to the temples. Aircraft overflights are currently a national issue and Air Tour Management Plans (ATMP) are being developed at some parks involving FAA and commercial tour operators.

KAHO: Kaloko-Honokohau National Histroic Park

Kaloko-Honokohau National Historical Park is located on the North Kona coast of the island of Hawai'i, about three miles north of Kailua and three miles south of the Kona International Airport. Hualalai volcano's 8,271-foot summit lies 10 miles east of the park. Containing 630 land acres and 500 water acres, the park provides a center for the preservation, interpretation, and perpetuation of traditional native Hawaiian activities and culture and preserves these resources in perpetuity. It makes the park a valuable part of America's heritage and is available to approximately 80,000 visitors each year for their experience, enjoyment, understanding, and appreciation.

The park is composed of 630 land acres and approximately 500 acres of offshore water in Honokohau Bay. The offshore water is under the jurisdiction of the State of Hawaii. The park area consists of those lands in the ahupua'a of Kaloko and Honokohau makai of the Queen Ka'ahumanu Highway. Included in the authorized boundary of the park are a coastal strip extending to Wawahiwa'a Point in the ahupua'a of Kohanaiki and two small parcels located in the ahupua'a of Kealakehe next to the Honokohau small boat harbor.

There is starkness to this landscape. Almost moonlike in its appearance, composed of geologically recent lava flows from Hualalai Volcano, the landscape looks harsh and incapable of supporting life. But there is plant and animal life here, and this land and its physical spirituality supported human life for at least a thousand years. The Hawaiian people who settled at Kaloko and Honokohau adapted to their natural surroundings, maintained balance in their use of food sources, and conducted their lives out of respect for the precariousness of survival.

Aimakapa Fishpond

Small permanent settlements probably developed on the leeward side of the island of Hawai'i sometime during the 10th and 11th centuries. These settlements would have grown near water, including the shallow bay of Kaloko. Fishponds were important shoreline features; the fish from these ponds were reserved for the ali'i (elite) and would have supplemented fish caught in the ocean. Fishponds provided a consistent and sustainable food source for the chief and his entourage as he traveled through his domain. Some inland bays, like Kaloko, were converted into ponds through the construction of stone walls with sluice gates. Such projects required prior planning, acquired engineering skills, strong social organization, and a massive labor pool.

Fishtrap

By contrast, a fishtrap is formed from a stone wall built from the shoreline to a protruding point of land. Examples of both exist within Kaloko-Honokohau NHP. It is believed that the Kaloko area supported a large population of both commoners and royalty, including members of the Kamehameha family (ohana). The Kaloko fishpond remained a working domestic and commercial fishpond until the early part of the 20th century.

Kaloko-Honokohau NHP contains portions of four ahupua'a (traditional Hawaiian land divisions), Kealakehe, Honokohau, Kaloko, and Kohanaiki. Each ahupua'a extended from sea to mountain and contained areas for fishing, living spaces with inshore marine resources and underground springs, crop production, timber cutting, and hunting. The Hawaiian people lived in self-sustaining communities with fresh and brackish water supplies, sea and fishpond harvests, and upland cultivation of sweet potatoes, taro, breadfruit, and coconuts. Early Hawaiians practiced environmental adaptation through the construction of the fishponds, agricultural planters and walled enclosures, and took advantage of the natural food sources. Subsistence activities were balanced with recreational and religious activities.

The fishpond developed in the park provides extremely rare and important habitat for water birds. The shoreline and fishponds not only contain endangered Hawaiian water birds such as Hawaiian stilt (ae'o) and Hawaiian coot (alaeke'ke'o), but also attract other migratory water birds as well. Kaloko and Honokohau represented life and spirituality not only in the past, but in the present and the future.

Hawaiians view the resources and cultural landscape in this park as supporting the perpetuation and renewal of Hawaiian culture and values. The park's resources, as a whole, represent a way of life and culture that still lives and contributes to national heritage.

Mission of National Park Service at Kaloko-Honokohau

The National Park Service at Kaloko-Honokohau National Historical Park provides a center for the preservation, interpretation, and perpetuation of traditional native Hawaiian activities and culture. The mission of the National Park Service at Kaloko-Honokohau is rooted in and grows from Public Law 95-625. Our mission statement is a synthesis of this mandated purpose, plus the park's primary significance as itemized below.

Legislative Intent

The law creating Kaloko-Honokohau (P.L. 95-625, 11/10/78) mandated the National Park Service to provide a center for the preservation, interpretation, and perpetuation of traditional native Hawaiian activities and culture and to demonstrate historic land use patterns as well as to provide a needed resource for the education, enjoyment, and appreciation of such traditional native Hawaiian activities and culture by local residents and visitors. On December 2, 2003, P.L. 108-142 was enacted to adjust the boundary of the park to add two adjacent parcels of land totaling 2.14 acres. One of the parcels includes a building that would be suitable to house administrative, interpretive, resource management, and maintenance functions.

Purpose

Kaloko-Honokohau is provides a place where native Hawaiians can practice historic and cultural traditions, thereby perpetuating an evolving culture. It provides education programs which instill an appreciation of traditional native Hawaiian activities and traditional land use patterns. It emphasizes the land-sea ethic, a dominant force in Hawaiian attitudes and feelings and demonstrated in traditional land use patterns. It protects and interprets archeological features and their cultural significance. The park also protects marine resources and habitat for threatened sea turtles and other marine species. Additionally it protects fishponds and habitat for endangered, native Hawaiian water birds.

Significance

The park is rich with archeological sites, including a full range of Hawaiian settlement features associated with both commoners and chiefs and features related to water/land use. The park's cultural landscape, as a whole, illustrates intangible values of Hawaiian culture including cooperation, social values, economies of scale, and advantages of specialization. Kaloko and 'Aimakapa fishponds and the 'Ai'opio fish trap illustrate ingenious Hawaiian construction and aquaculture techniques and provide wetland habitat for endangered endemic Hawaiian water birds (the stilt, ae'o and the coot, 'alaeke'oke'o). Water served as a life force in the ahupua'a of Kaloko and Honokohau in many ways. Fresh water was scarce and invaluable and while water of the ocean and fishponds provided a rich source of food. Kaloko-Honokohau NHP has spiritual power, mana, offering a place for renewal of Hawaiian spiritual and cultural values.

Key External Factors

While park management and staff can plan, manage, and largely control much of what occurs in the park, other things they can only influence, especially things external to park boundaries. Some things, such as natural events, they have no control over whatsoever. In developing Kaloko-Honokohau's Strategic Plan and its long-term goals, it was important to take into consideration key external factors that could negatively or positively affect goal outcomes. A few of the most important or most likely are identified briefly below. This is by no means an exhaustive list but simply those that are most likely to influence outcomes as viewed at the time of writing the plan.

Recreational Fee Demonstration and the Federal Lands Recreation Enhancement Act
In 1996, Congress created the Recreational Fee Demonstration Program, which allows participating parks to retain 80 percent of the revenue collected through recreational fees. The remaining 20% is distributed throughout the Service to all parks, including those parks not actively collecting fees. Kaloko-Honokohau National Historical Park participates in the Recreational Fee Demonstration Program as a 20% park.

The Federal Lands Recreation Enhancement Act (FLREA) was passed in the 2005 Omnibus Appropriations bill signed into law By President Bush on December 8, 2004 to provide 10-year recreation fee authority to the Departments of Interior and Agriculture. As under the Recreational Fee Demonstration Program, FLREA benefits visitors to Federal public lands by reinvesting a majority of fees back to the site of collection to enhance visitor services and reducing the backlog of maintenance needs for recreational facilities. FLREA lists specific types of expenditures that would be permitted under Section 8(a)(3)(A-F) of the law:

Section 8(a)(3)(A) "Repair, maintenance, and facility enhancement related directly to visitor enjoyment, visitor access, and health and safety"

Section 8(a)(3)(B) "Interpretation, visitor information, visitor service, visitor needs assessments, and signs"

Section 8(a)(3)(C) "Habitat restoration directly related to wildlife-dependent recreation that is limited to hunting, fishing, wildlife observation, or photography"

Section 8(a)(3)(D) "Law enforcement related to public use and recreation"

Section 8(a)(3)(E) "Direct operating or capital costs associated with the recreation fee program"

Section 8(a)(3)(F) "A fee management agreement established under section 6(a) or a visitor reservation service"

The cultural resources preservation program at Kaloko-Honokohau National Historical Park has benefited greatly from the Recreational Fee Demonstration Program. The restoration of the sea wall at Kaloko fishpond is being partially funded through the program. The Recreational Fee Demonstration Program has brought a much-needed influx of new funds into park areas. The continuation of the program as the Federal Lands Recreation Enhancement Act is essential to maintain the momentum that we have gained in addressing backlogged maintenance, providing for interpretation projects, and preserving park resources for visitor enjoyment.

Adjacent Land Uses
Future Park planning needs to be done in a regional context because of its location next to an expanding urbanized area. What is happening on lands around the park must be taken into consideration. Over the past two decades, major changes in land use have occurred in the vicinity of Kaloko-Honokohau. The coming decades promise even greater changes will take place on these adjacent lands. They will no longer be open spaces and unoccupied lands. Light industrial development has already occurred on some of the mauka lands, and there are plans for much more development to the north and south of the park; resorts, residential housing, commercial and governmental centers, educational facilities, all part of the plan to make nearby Kailua town a major future urban growth area for the island of Hawai'i.

The study report, Spirit of Kaloko-Honokohau, calls for the use of the traditional Hawaiian ahupua'a concept of land use in securing off-site controls to ensure that the integrity of the Kaloko-Honokohau is maintained. The study report stated that the State of Hawai'i should be prevailed upon to keep much of the area around the then proposed park in the Conservation

District classification. Unfortunately, in the intervening years, the opposite has already occurred and much of the land around Kaloko-Honokohau has been reclassified from the Conservation to the Urban District to pave the way for future development.

Adjacent urban development, housing, small boat harbor expansion, oil/fuel line development, increased traffic along the major highway and increased highway capacity threatened park resources. Increased pressure on potable water sources might adversely affect the aquatic water ecosystems. Vital resources are at risk from the lack of community sewage system adjacent to park lands.

Visitor use patterns are strongly influenced by the Hawaiian tourism industry and are closely tied to each island's long range economic development plans. These externally influenced use patterns strongly impact the ability of the park's staff and infrastructure to accommodate the visitors when they arrive in the park.

The economic base of the Island of Hawaii is in transition. New economic options are being pursued. The park must play a role in ensuring that any economic endeavor adjacent to the park does not become a threat to the park and its resources.

PUHO: Pu'uhonua O Honaunau National Historic Park

Pu'uhonua o Honaunau National Historical Park is located on the South Kona coast of the island of Hawai'i and contains about 420 acres of federal lands, including a 3.7 acre detached upland parcel with no off-shore waters within its boundaries. The park protects, preserves and interprets significant sites and objects associated with the Pu'uhonua o Honaunau (the place of refuge at Honaunau) in perpetuity and makes this valuable part of America's heritage available to over 500,000 visitors each year for their experience, enjoyment, understanding, and appreciation. On the black lava flats of the southern Kona Coast, the park preserves aspects of traditional Hawaiian life.

Honaunau Bay, with its sheltered canoe landing and availability of drinking water, was a natural place for the chiefs, ali'i, to establish one of their most important residences. The Hawaiian concept of a sanctuary, pu'uhonua, offering people a second chance at life is the primary story at this park. In the centuries before 1819, Hawaiian people caught in extraordinary circumstances, such as being on the losing side in war, being defeated in battle, or breaking sacred laws, kapu, could escape the death sentence if they could physically get to the pu'uhonua. A priest, kahuna pule, would perform a ceremony of absolution and the defeated warrior or law breaker could return home safely.

In addition to being the site of a pu'uhonua, the ahupua'a of Honaunau was the residence of ruling chiefs of Kona. With its bountiful food and drinking water supplies, Honaunau supported both royalty and commoners. Visitors to the park today can feel the mana of this sacred place. Park lands contain the coastal areas of two ahupua'a: Honaunau and Keokea, and coastal and upland areas of Ki'ilae ahupua'a. Time periods represented by the park's resources include pre-contact, contact, and post-contact to the abolition of kapu in 1819, removal of ali'i remains from the Hale o Keawe heiau in late 1828-early 1829, and the abandonment of Ki'ilae Village in the 1930s.

Through the years, surveys of cultural resources have recorded 321 archeological and historical features and structures within the park, representing almost all aspects of early Hawaiian life. Most of these features are located toward the sea, makai, of the 1871 Trail; from Alahaka to Ki'ilae the features are located mauka, or inland. The entire area surrounding the refuge and royal grounds was densely settled and now contains significant archeological remains.

Honaunau was the site of a pu'uhonua and was the original seat of the chiefdom of Kona and the ancestral home of the Kamehameha dynasty. The ruling chief and his court occupied dwelling areas at the head of Honaunau Bay and along the shore to the south. The homes of lesser chiefs and of common people were on the north shore of Honaunau Bay and at Ki'ilae Village. Access to the pu'uhonua would have been from the south by land, or by the bay from the north. The presence of the royal grounds would have prohibited entry from the east.

Mission of National Park Service at Pu'uhonua o Honaunau
The National Park Service at Pu'uhonua o Honaunau National Historical Park protects, preserves, and interprets for the benefit and inspiration of the people and future generations, the nationally significant sites and objects associated with the pu'uhonua o Honaunau (the place of refuge at Honaunau).

Legislative Intent
City of Refuge National Historical Park was authorized by Congress on July 26, 1955 (69 Stat. 385), accomplished by secretarial order effective July 1, 1961, supplemented with the official name change to Pu'uhonua o Honaunau National Historical Park in 1978 (P. L. 95-625), and codified in Title 16 of the United States Code, section 397. The law creating the park mandated the Secretary of the Interior to: "set apart as the City of Refuge National Historical Park, in the Territory of Hawaii, for the benefit and inspiration of the people."

The entire park was listed on the National Register of Historic Places on October 15, 1977. The park's boundaries coincided with the national register nomination boundaries. On December 16, 2002 (P.L. 107-340), Congress modified the park's boundaries to include 238 acres of land which contains the remnants of an ancient Hawaiian village (Ki'ilae), a small portion of which has recently been included within the park's boundary. Funding for the acquisition of the lands within the modified boundaries was included in the National Park Service's FY-05 appropriations. Title to the above parcel of land passed from The Trust for Public Land to the United States of America on August 30, 2006.

Purpose
The purpose of Pu'uhonua o Honaunau NHP is to preserve, protect, restore, and maintain natural resources and significant archaeological sites associated with Pu'uhonua o Honaunau NHP. It interprets the cultural values, traditions, and human story associated with the pu'uhonua. This provides an understanding of, and inspiration for, the Hawaiian cultural values associated with these sites. Additionally it is a place where native Hawaiians can practice cultural traditions.

Significance
The pu'uhonua is the best preserved existing historical feature that illustrates the association of the Hawaiian lifestyle and kapu system. It includes the site of the Hawaiian royal

residences/compound. The park is of religious and cultural importance to the Hawaiian community and is still used today for traditional cultural activities. Hale o Keawe is the finest example of a temple used to house the bones of sacred chiefs. Pu'uhonua o Honaunau NHP contains the most massive wall built in pre-contact Hawai'i. Pu'uhonua o Honaunau NHP has an association with several generations of high-ranking chiefs, including Kamehameha the Great. The village of Ki'ilae is an intact archaeological site, dating from pre-contact to the 1830s, illustrating aspects of Hawaiian daily life.

Key External Factors

While park management and staff can plan, manage, and largely control much of what occurs in the park, other things they can only influence, especially things external to park boundaries. Some things, such as natural events, they have no control over whatsoever. In developing Pu'uhonua o Honaunau's Strategic Plan and its long term goals, it was important to take into consideration key external factors that could negatively or positively affect goal outcomes. A few of the most important or most likely to induce change are identified briefly below. This is by no means an exhaustive list but simply those that are most likely to influence outcomes as viewed at the time of writing the plan.

In 1996, Congress created the Recreational Fee Demonstration Program, which allows participating parks to retain 80 percent of the revenue collected through recreational fees. The Recreational Fee Demonstration Program has brought a much-needed influx of new funds into park areas. The continuation of the program was essential to maintain the momentum that we have gained in addressing backlogged maintenance, providing for interpretation projects, and preserving park resources.

The Federal Lands Recreation Enhancement Act (FLREA) was passed in the 2005 Omnibus Appropriations bill signed into law by President Bush on December 8, 2004 to provide 10-year recreation fee authority to the Departments of Interior and Agriculture. As under the Recreational Fee Demonstration Program, FLREA benefits visitors to Federal public lands by reinvesting a majority of fees back to the site of collection to enhance visitor services and reducing the backlog of maintenance needs for recreational facilities. FLREA lists specific types of expenditures that would be permitted under Section 8(a)(3)(A-F) of the law:

Section 8(a)(3)(A) "Repair, maintenance, and facility enhancement related directly to visitor enjoyment, visitor access, and health and safety"

Section 8(a)(3)(B) "Interpretation, visitor information, visitor service, visitor needs assessments, and signs"

Section 8(a)(3)(C) "Habitat restoration directly related to wildlife-dependent recreation that is limited to hunting, fishing, wildlife observation, or photography"

Section 8(a)(3)(D) "Law enforcement related to public use and recreation"

Section 8(a)(3)(E) "Direct operating or capital costs associated with the recreation fee program"

Section 8(a)(3)(F) "A fee management agreement established under section 6(a) or a visitor reservation service"

The Recreational Fee Demonstration Program has brought a much-needed influx of new funds into park areas. The continuation of the program as the Federal Lands Recreation Enhancement Act is essential to maintain the momentum that we have gained in addressing backlogged maintenance, providing for interpretation projects, and preserving park resources for visitor enjoyment.

Adjacent Land Uses

Land use in the Island of Hawaii is in a state of change. The island was predominantly agriculture oriented; however, there has been a gradual shift toward land development for the visitor industry as well as the development of retirement or second home communities.

Current land use surrounding Pu'uhonua o Honaunau has the potential for change. The Honaunau Bay area north of the park is inhabited by a few families who lease the land from Kamehameha Schools/Bishop Estate in addition to those who own their own land. The last decade has seen a dramatic growth in tourist facilities in Kona, although, thus far, it has not progressed south of Kealakekua Bay. The future, however, suggests possible development on these coastal lands, including hotels, vacation homes, and all the attendant roads, shops, restaurants, utilities, and other facilities.

Although the extent of future development is not known, it is still likely that land around the park, which is now open space, will someday support developments similar to that between Keauhou Bay and Kailua. The park must play a role in ensuring that any economic endeavor adjacent to the park does not become a threat to the park and its resources.

Appendix B. Revision History Log

Changes to the SOPs will be logged here. Version numbers increase incrementally by hundredths (e.g., version 1.01, version 1.02) for minor changes. Major revisions should be designated with the next whole number (e.g., version 2.0, 3.0, 4.0). Record the previous version number, date of revision, author of the revision; identify paragraphs and pages where changes are made, who approved the revision, and the reason for making the changes along with the new version number.

Previous Version #	Revision Date	Author	Changes Made	Reason for Change	New Version #

Appendix C. Permits and Permission

Various environmental permits and compliance procedures are required to implement this monitoring. As this protocol is implemented, we will proceed through project compliance as appropriate for each park according to federal as well as for state/commonwealth/territory guidelines. We will ensure full compliance with all existing and future regulations.

Permits

Federal

NPS: NPS research permits will be obtained, in advance of any field activities, for each park where monitoring occurs. Permits will be evaluated on an annual basis, or other timeframe as stipulated in the permit itself. The research permit review process also includes NEPA compliance documentation, as discussed further below. The PI and Bio-tech will maintain all appropriate documentation.

NEPA: At present, under the National Environmental Policy Act (NEPA), we anticipate that this protocol falls under a Categorical Exclusion (CE) where "a category of actions which do not individually or cumulatively have a significant effect …and for which, therefore, neither an environmental assessment nor an environmental impact statement is required" (40 CFR 1508.4). Under Directors Order 12 a CE (or CX) is "an action with no measurable environmental impact which is described in one of the categorical exclusion lists in section 3.3 or 3.4 and for which no exceptional circumstances (section 3.5) exist." NEPA compliance review and documentation will occur as part of the NPS research permitting process.

State, Territorial, and Commonwealth

State of Hawaii: Department of Land and Natural Resources, the Division of Aquatic Resources issues permits, including scientific research (http://www.state.hi.us/dlnr/dar/licenses.htm, accessed 14 April 2008). The application to apply for a special activity permit can be downloaded online and must be submitted either by mail or fax at least 2 weeks prior to the start of research. The permit will be issued to the Principal Investigator and must list all individuals who will take part in the scientific collection.

Territory of American Samoa: The territory requires a permit through the Department of Marine and Wildlife Resources.

Village permission should be obtained by personally contacting the village mayor to describe what the study is about, prior to initiating any work.

Commonwealth of the Northern Mariana Islands: CNMI requires a permit through the Coastal Resources Management Office. A CRM research application can be found at http://www.crm.gov.mp/programs/permitting/app.asp.

Permission should also be obtained from the CNMI Division of Fish and Wildlife. An application for a scientific permit can be found at http://www.dfw.gov.mp/planning/planfs.htm.

Compliance

Compliance Procedures as currently recommended by the PACN I&M Steering Committee.

1) I&M is the proponent of work within the parks and initiates compliance for each protocol in each park. Each park uses its own compliance method.

2) I&M applies for a Research Permit with each park where monitoring will be conducted, and the park's compliance coordinator/specialist decides whether the Permit is adequate.

3) I&M fills out the Environmental Screening Form in PEPC for those parks that will require it and also saves it as a Word document; parks that don't use PEPC can use the Word version if needed.

4) I&M will not begin any work in a park until the park-specific process has been followed, and the approval is signed off in appropriate forms.

5) I&M proceeds with initiation of compliance as soon as a protocol's development is sufficient, even if implementation is scheduled for later on.

6) Continue as necessary per individual park requirements.

Appendix D. Sampling Frame

The following maps describe the sampling frame for each of the parks in the PACN. These maps will be updated with fixed sites once these sites are determined and established. Within each park are listed the freshwater, brackish, and marine water targeted for monitoring in this protocol.

Figures

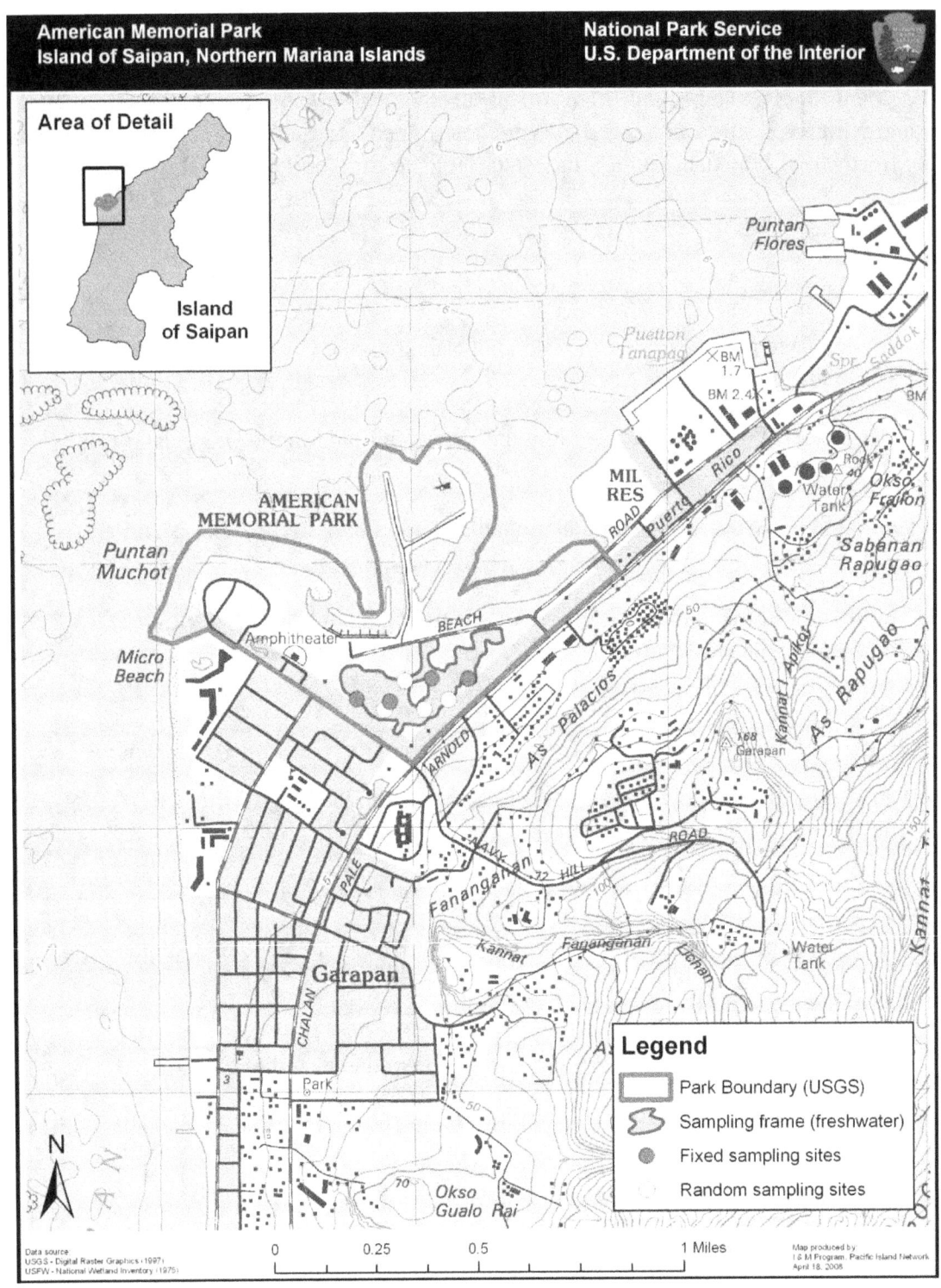

Figure D1. American Memorial Park on the island of Saipan in the Commonwealth of the Northern Marianna Islands. The wetland is part of the freshwater sampling frame.

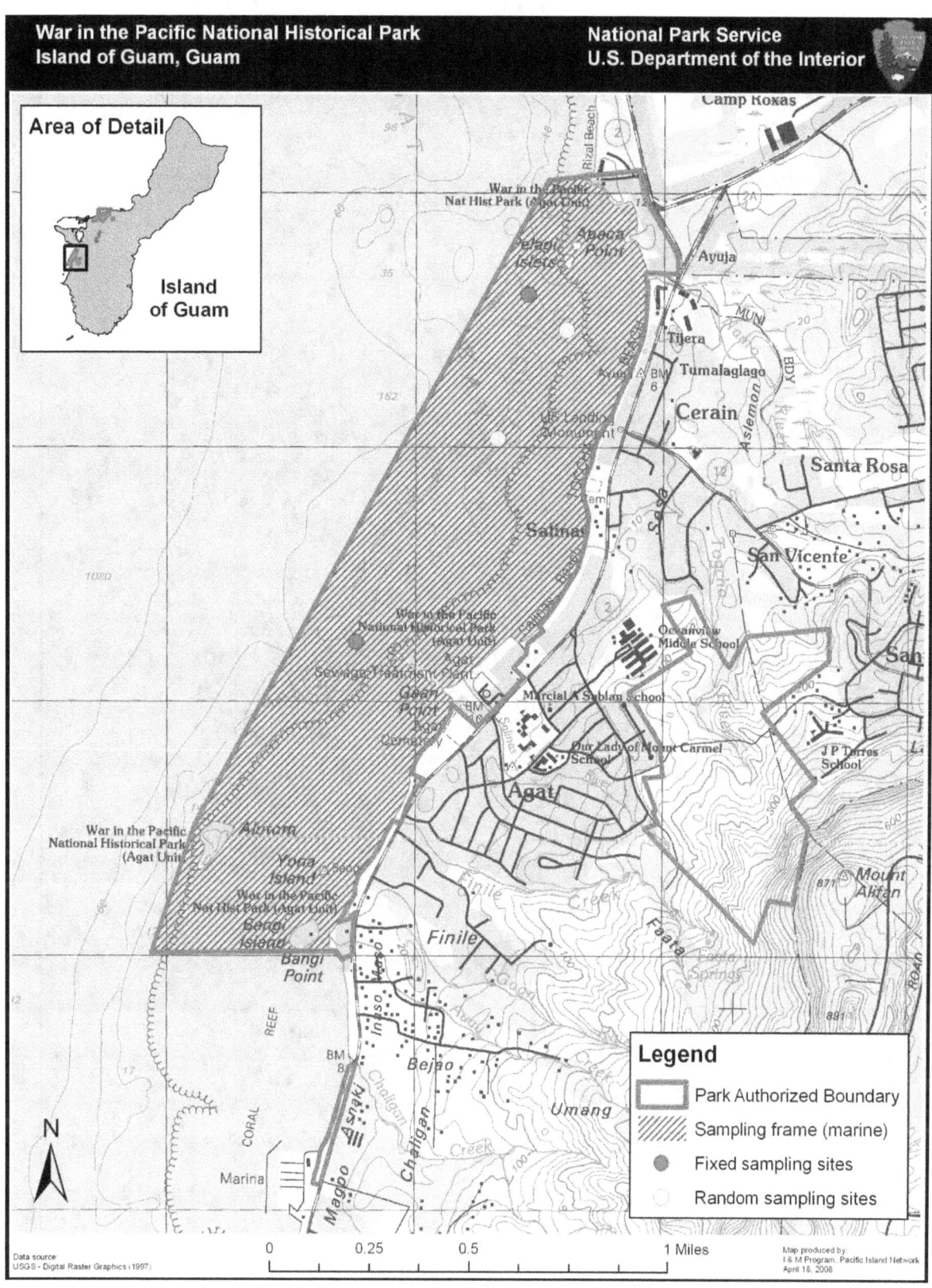

Legend

☐ Park Authorized Boundary

▧ Sampling frame (marine)

● Fixed sampling sites

○ Random sampling sites

Figure D2 .Agat unit of War in the Pacific National Historical Park on the U.S. island territory of Guam. This sampling frame unit of WAPA contains only marine water.

31

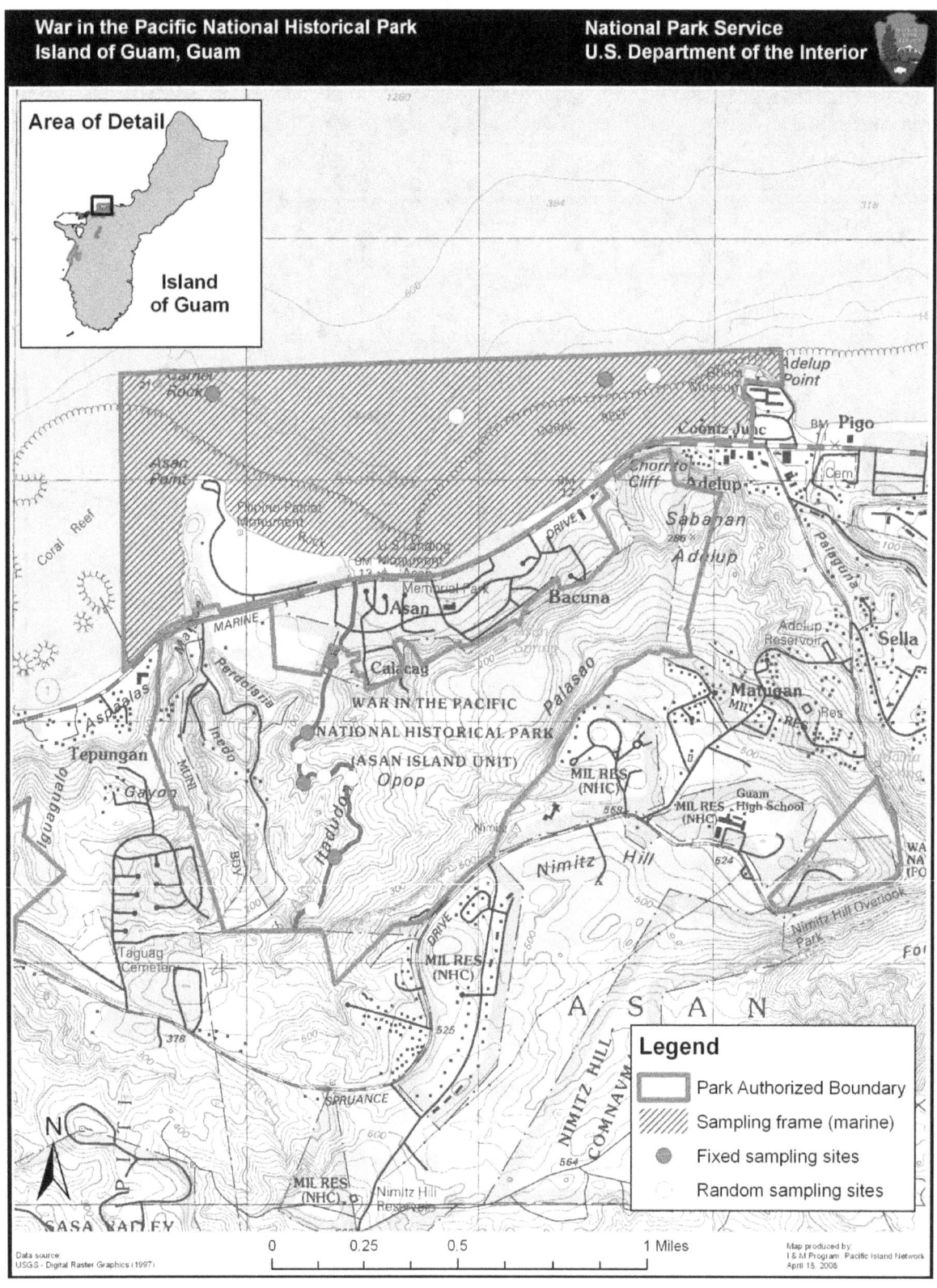

Legend

☐ Park Authorized Boundary

▨ Sampling frame (marine)

● Fixed sampling sites

○ Random sampling sites

Figure D3. Asan unit of War in the Pacific National Historical Park on the U.S. island territory of Guam. This sampling frame unit of WAPA contains marine and freshwater resources.

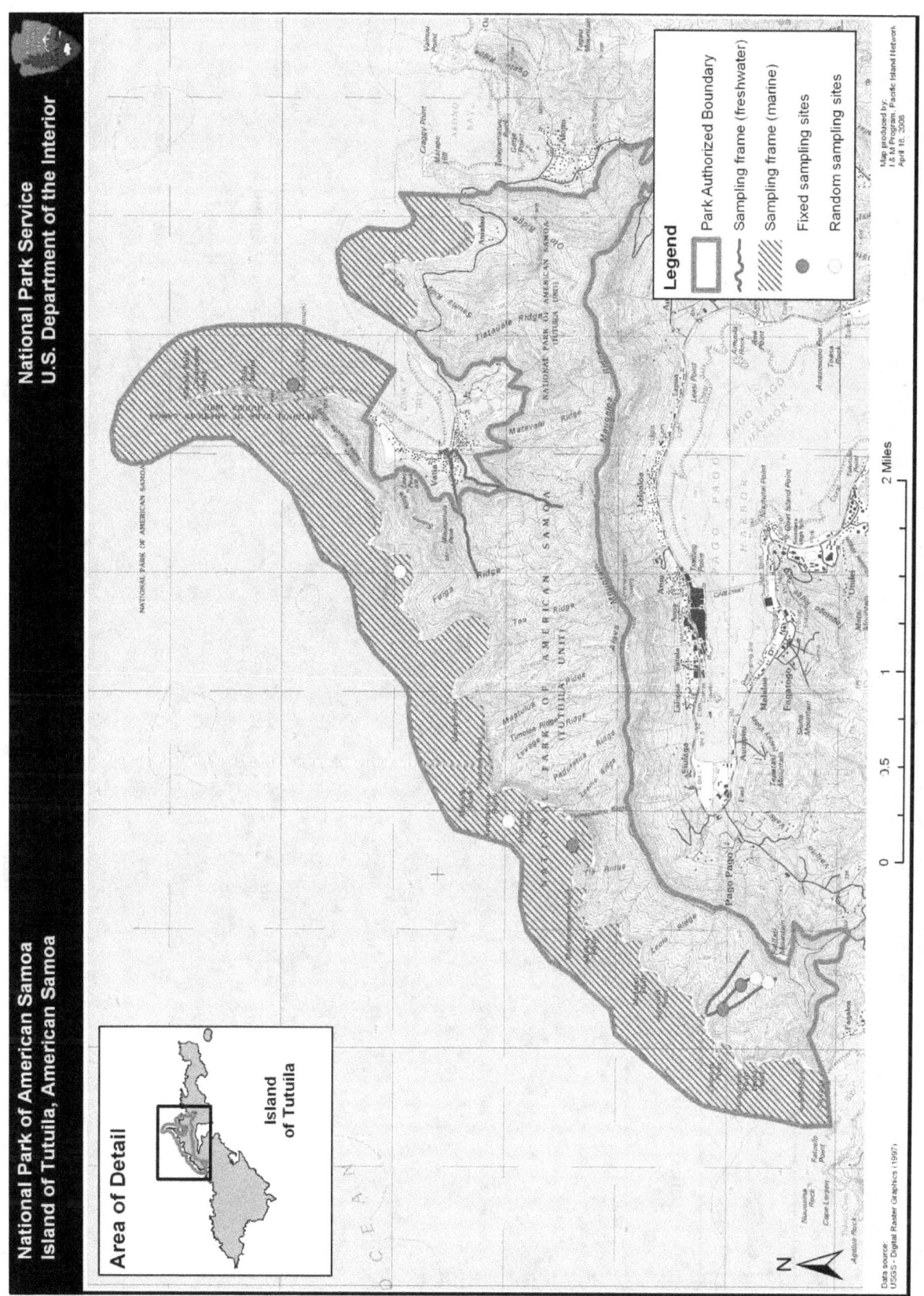

Figure D4. Tutuila unit of the National Park of American Samoa in the U.S. territory of American Samoa on the island of Tutuila. This sampling frame unit of NPSA contains marine and freshwater resources.

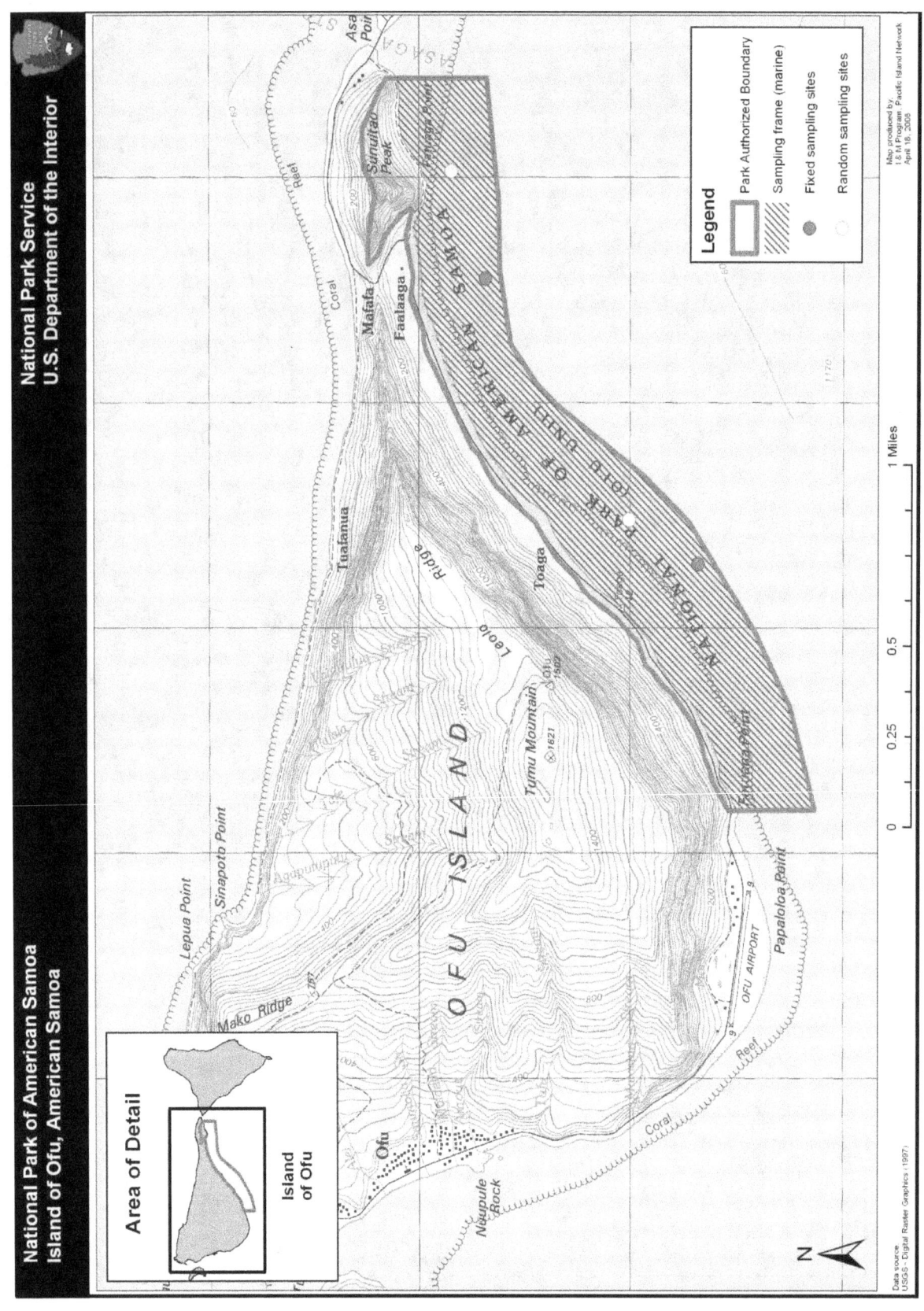

Figure D5. Ofu unit of the National Park of American Samoa in the U.S. territory of American Samoa on the island of Ofu. This sampling frame unit of NPSA contains only marine resources.

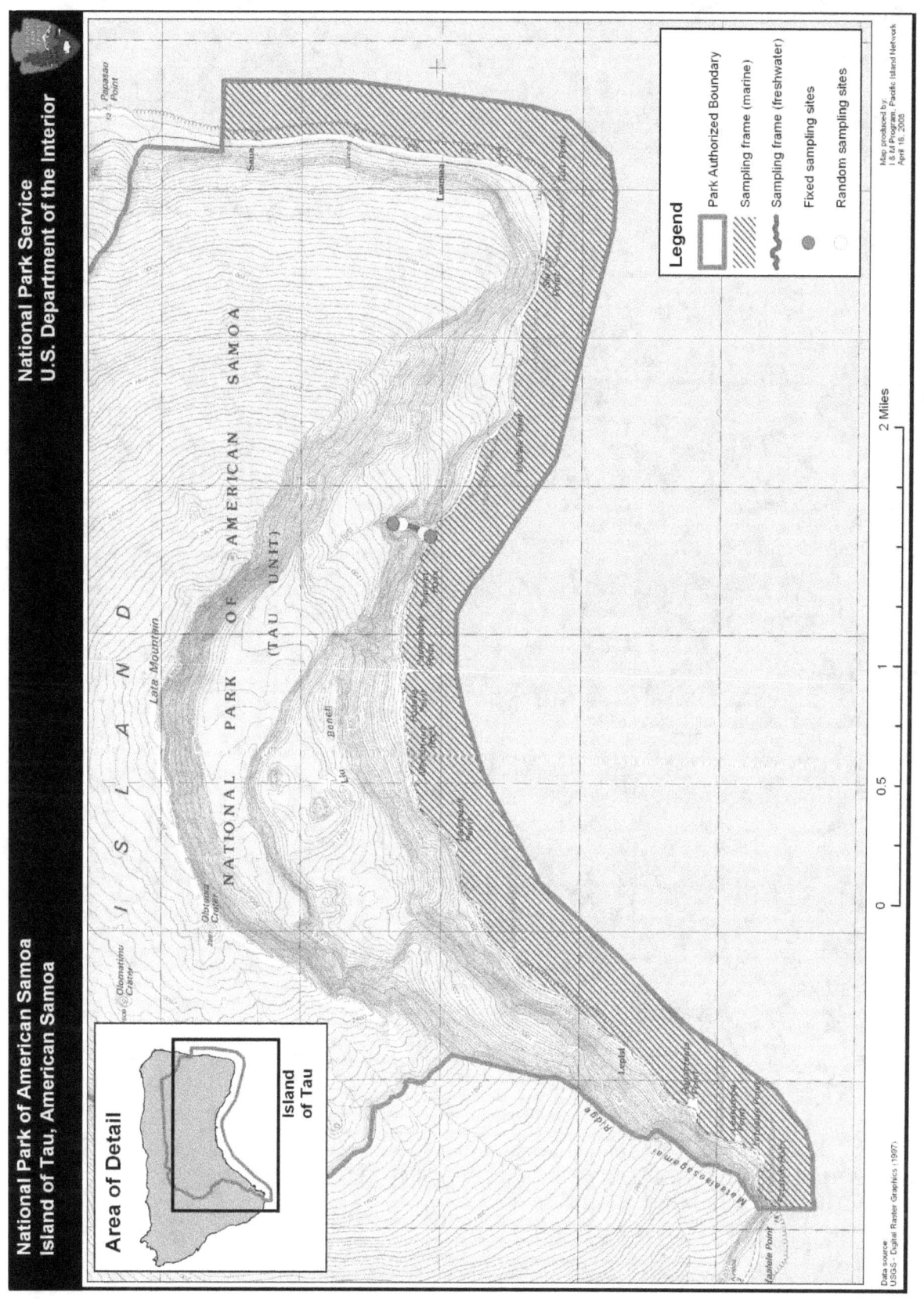

Figure D6. Tau unit of the National Park of American Samoa in the U.S. territory of American Samoa on the island of Tau. This sampling frame unit of NPSA contains marine and freshwater resources. Only freshwater will be monitored initially.

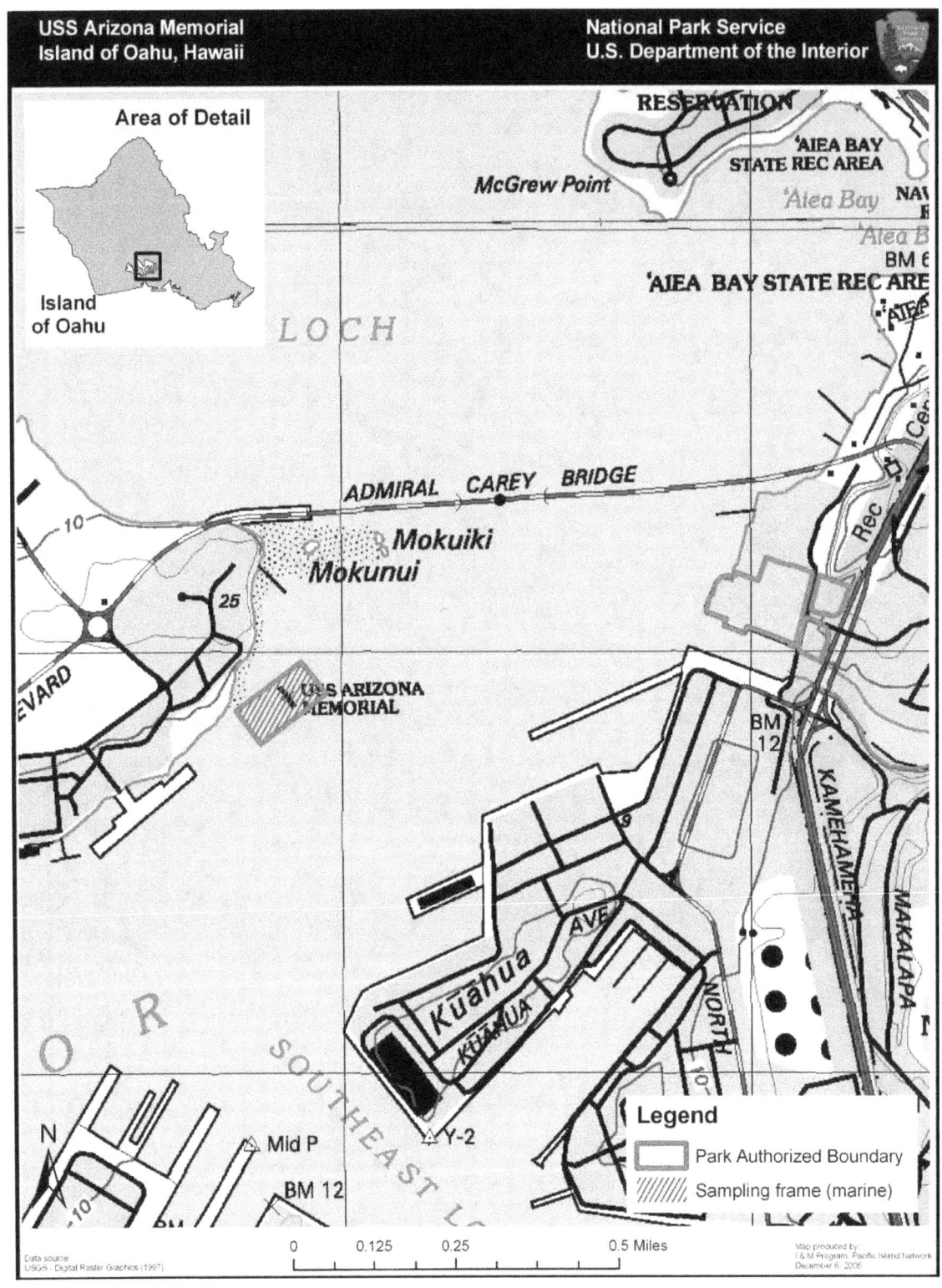

Figure D7. The USS Arizona Memorial on the Hawaiian island of Oahu. This park will not be monitored by the PACN Water Quality Monitoring protocol.

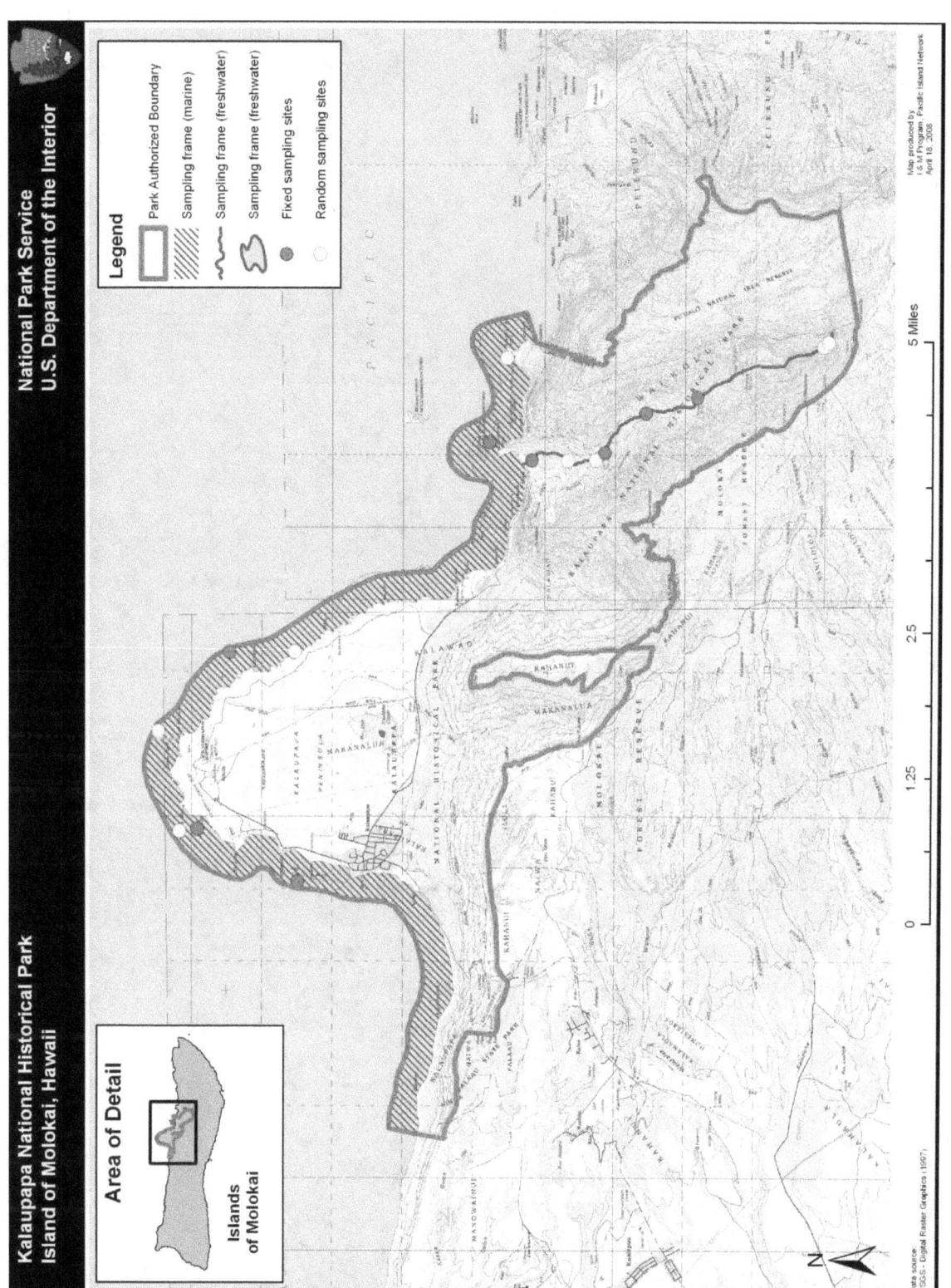

Figure D8. The Kalaupapa National Historical Park on the Hawaiian island of Molokai. The sampling frame in KALA contains freshwater, and marine resources.

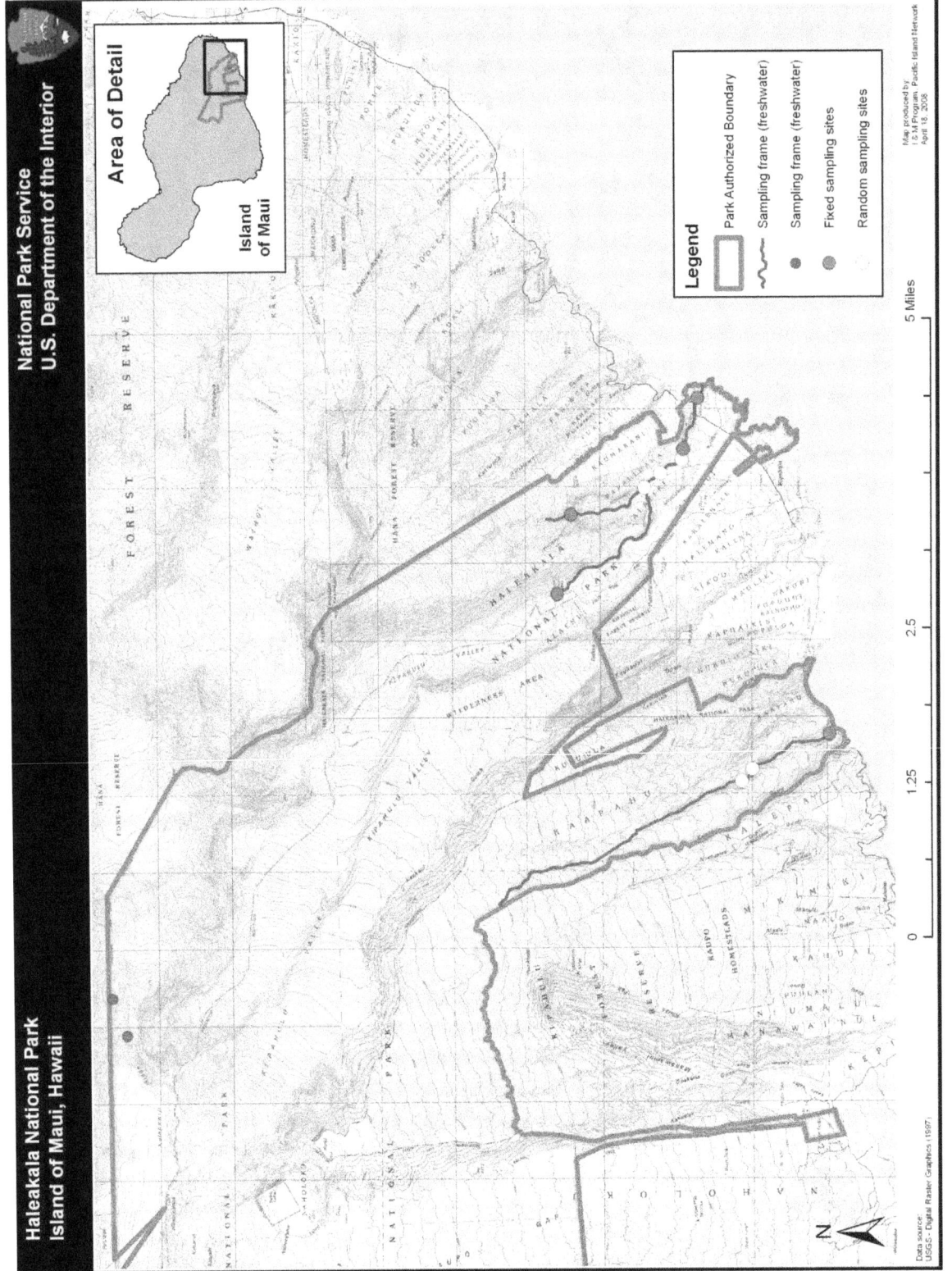

Figure D9. Haleakala National Park on the Hawaiian island of Maui. The sampling frame in HALE contains only freshwater resources.

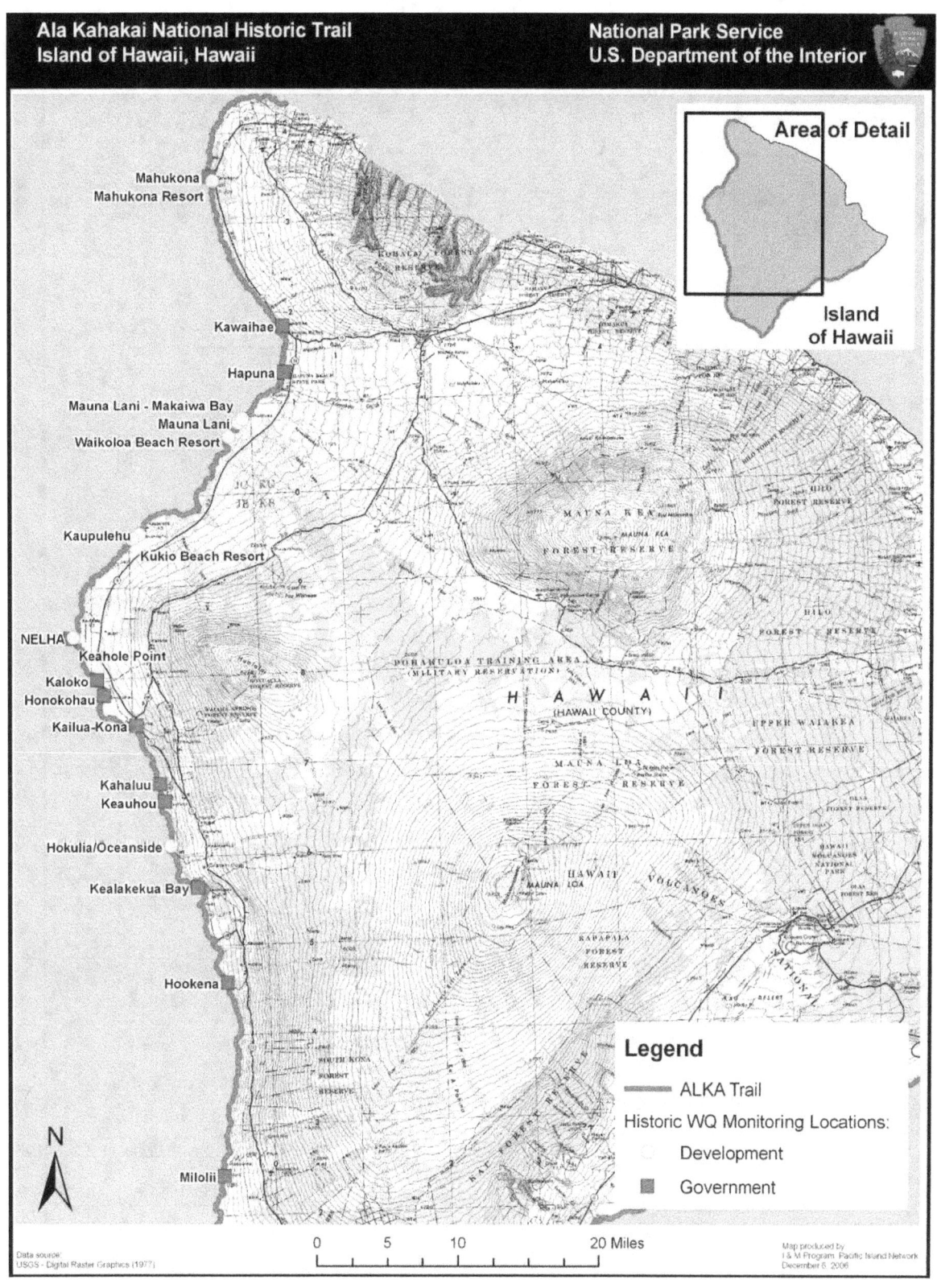

Figure D10. Ala Kahakai National Historic Trail on the Hawaiian island of Hawaii. Sampling along ALKA is being conducted by various groups and agencies and will only be monitored at specified critical monitoring points along the trail using this Water Quality protocol.

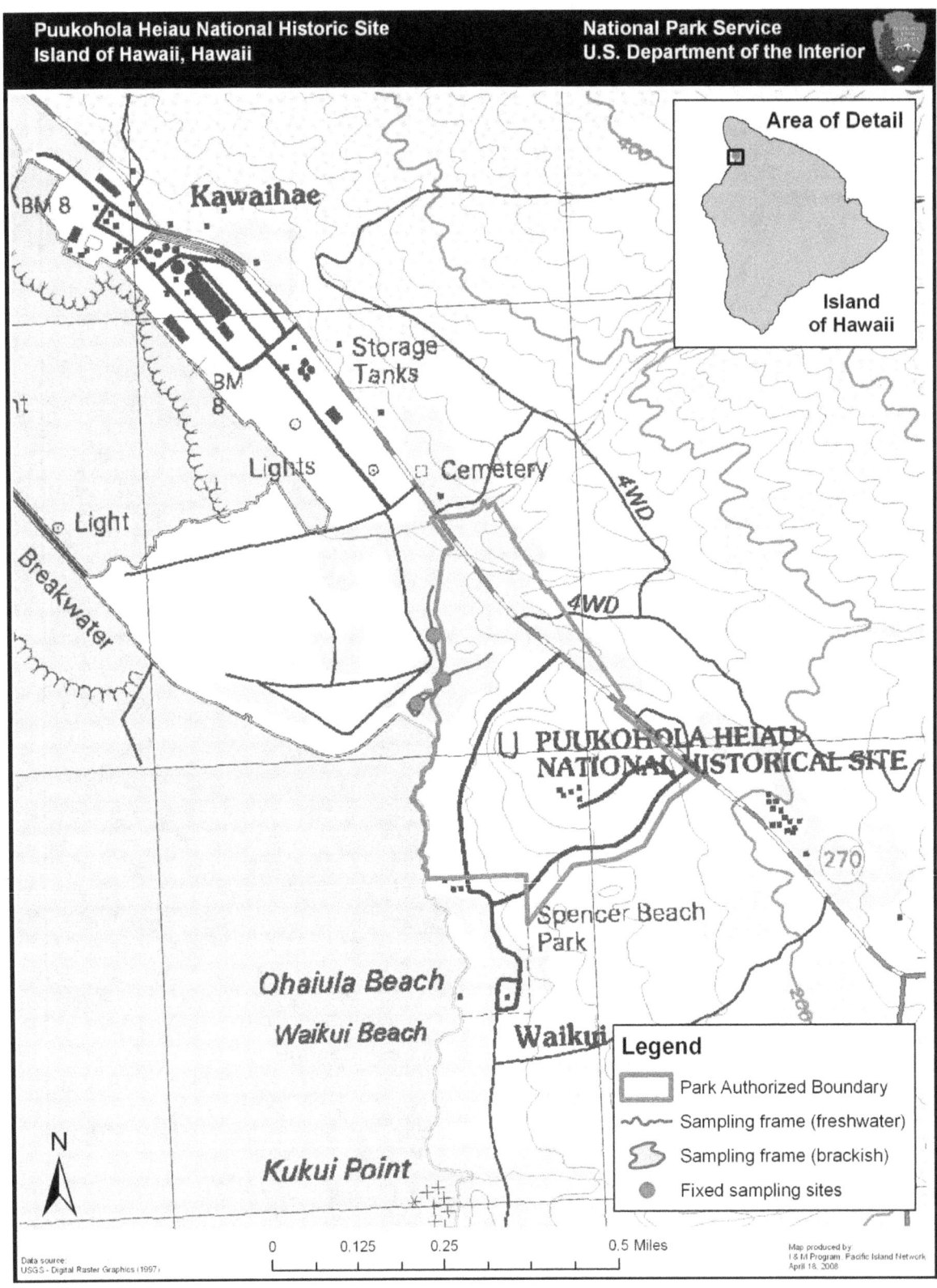

Figure D11. Puukohola Heiau National Historic Site on the Hawaiian island of Hawaii. The sampling frame in PUHE contains only freshwater resources.

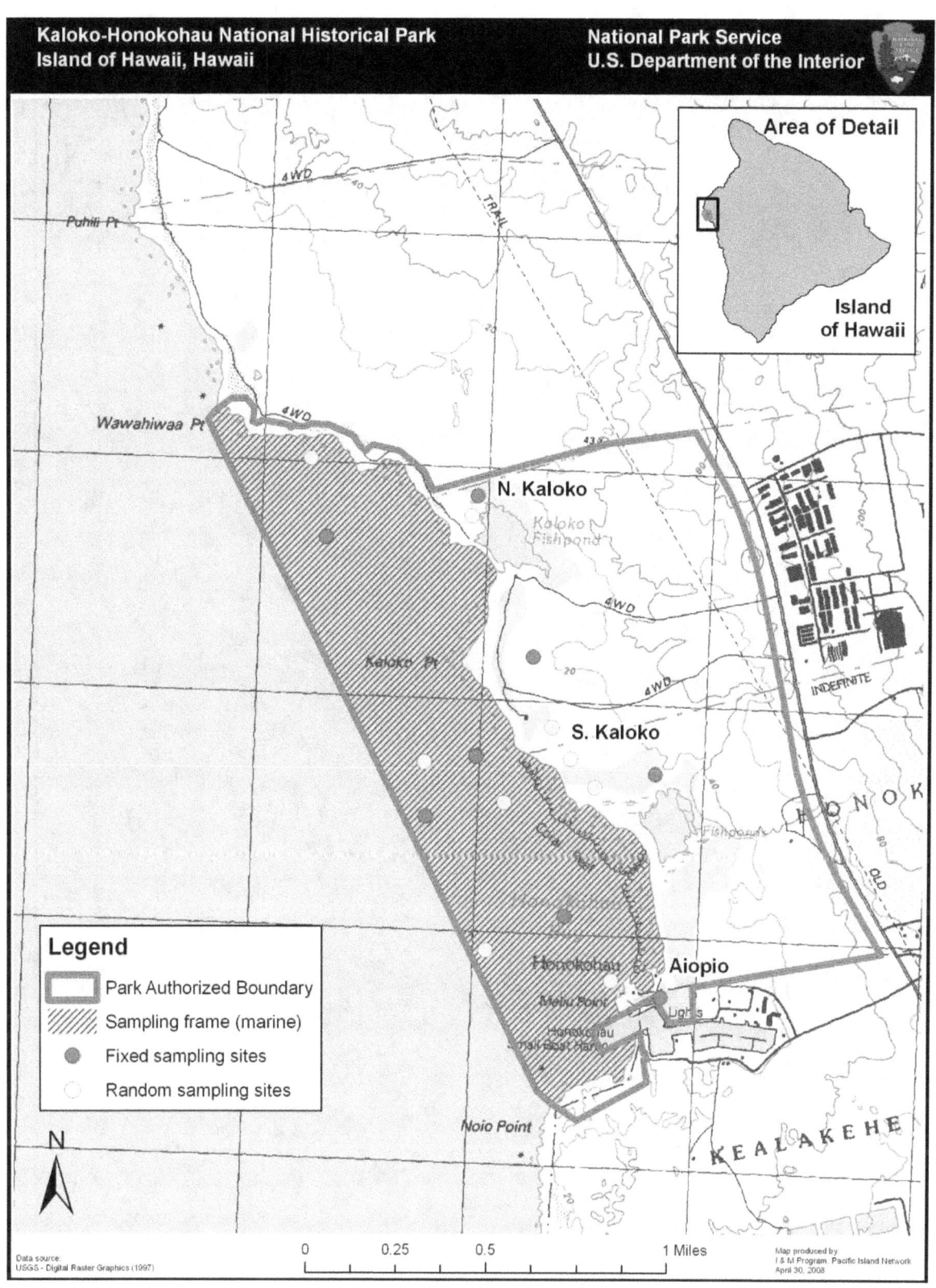

Figure D12. Kaloko-Honokohau National Historical Park on the Hawaiian island of Hawaii. The sampling frame in KAHO contains marine and brackish water resources (anchialine pools).

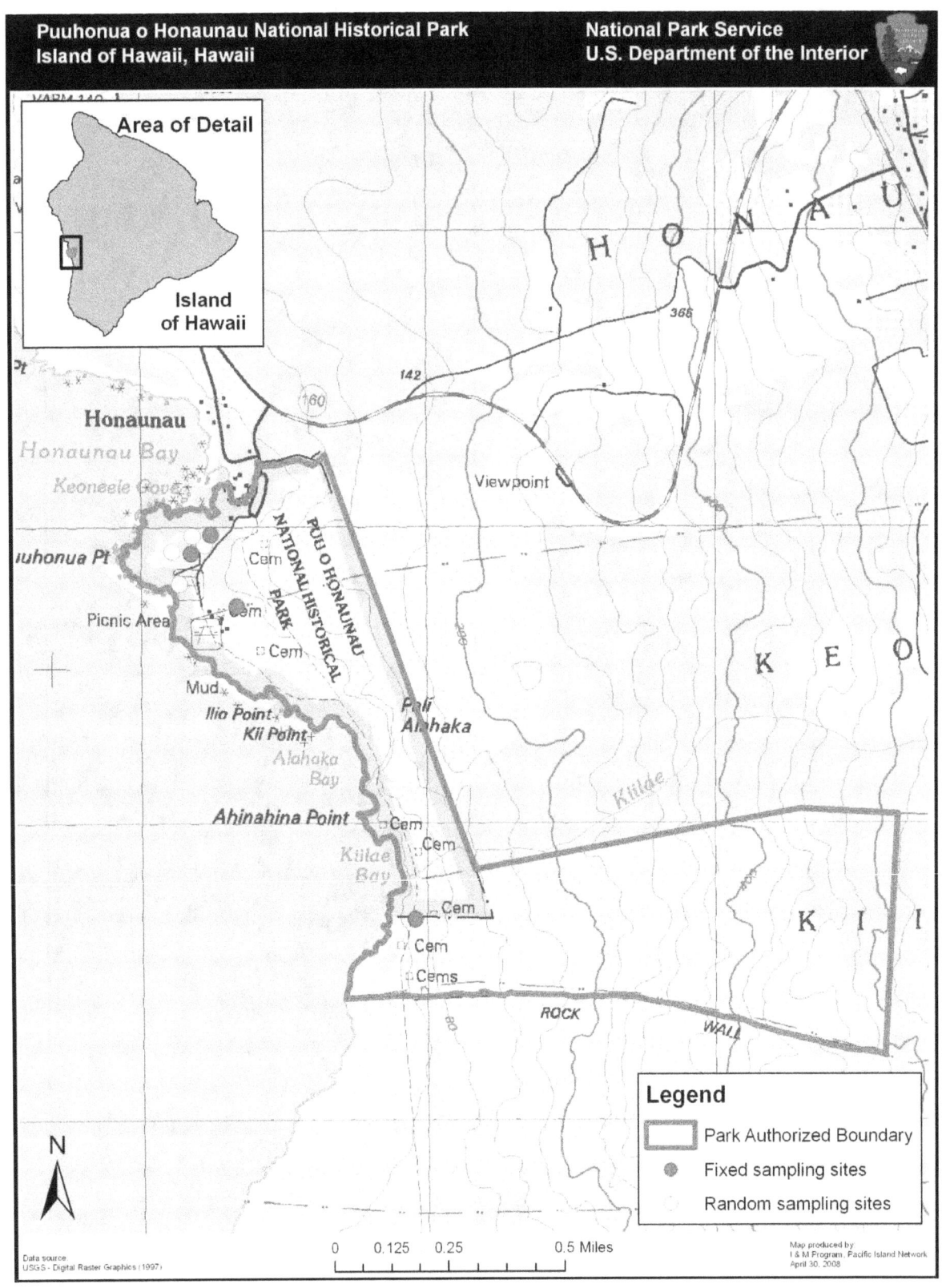

Figure D13. Puuhonua o Honaunau National Historical Park on the Hawaiian island of Hawaii. The sampling frame in PUHO contains only brackish water resources (anchialine pools).

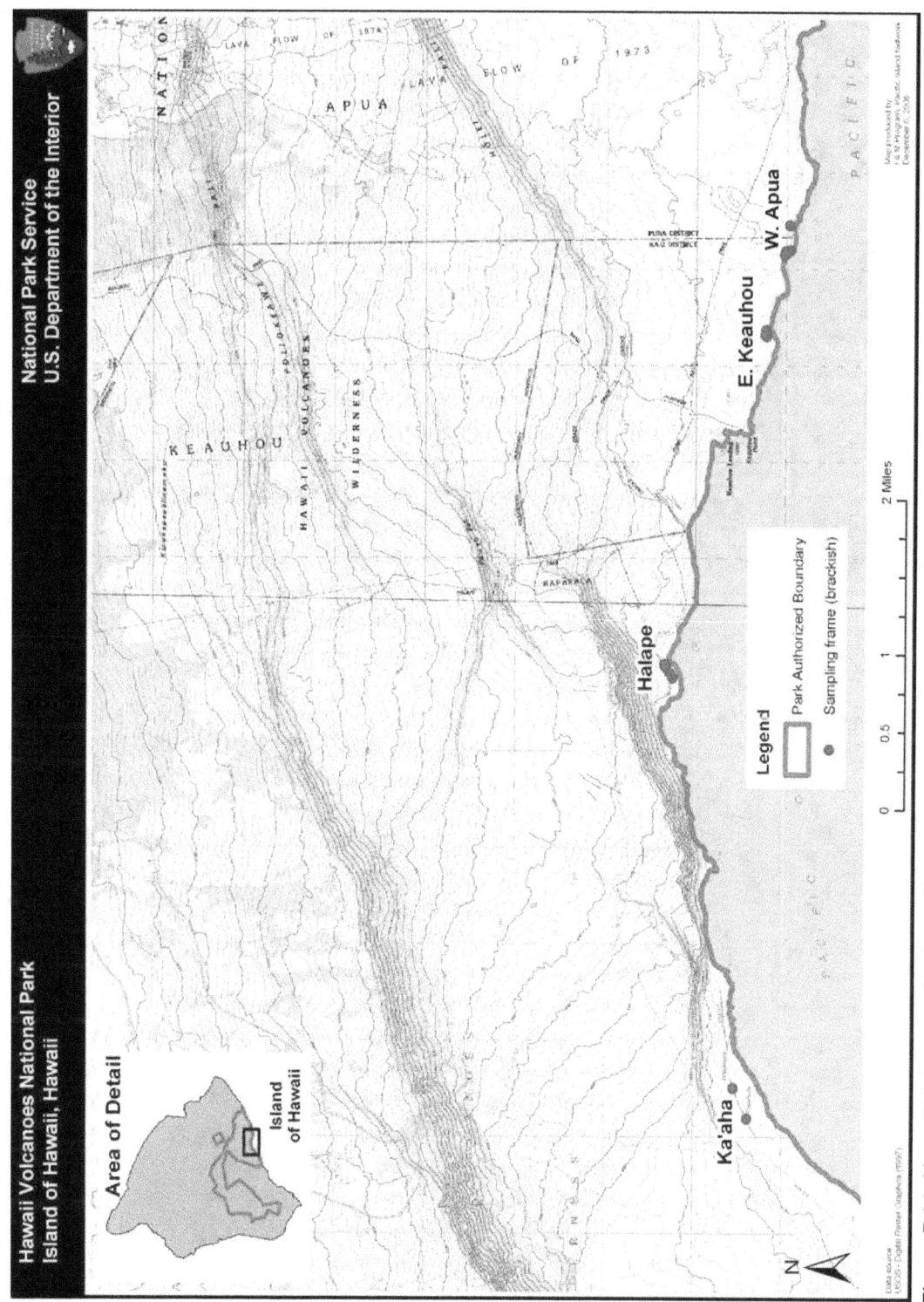

Figure D14. Hawaii Volcanoes National Park on the Hawaiian island of Hawaii. The sampling frame in HAVO contains only brackish water resources (anchialine pools).

Appendix E. Field Data Form

Date:	Park:	Station Number:	Names:

Station Type (circle)	Time	Resource Type (circle):	
Fixed site Random site	s: e:	Marine Brackish Freshwater	

Site location:	Latitude		Longitude	Error ±

Environmental Conditions (circle):					Wind Direction (N/E/W/S)	Wind Force Beaufort
Sunny (≥75% sun)	Partly Cloudy (≥25% and ≤75% sun)	Mostly Cloudy (≤25% sun)	Overcast	Rain		

Digital Photograph Information:	Picture #	Direction	Comments: This is a required picture of the sampling site
Picture # Direction Comments			

Water Condition Assesment: (Circle or estimate)		Tidal Stage	Direction	Wave Height (Estimated)
		High	Ebb	
Flow Level: Dry No Flow	Low	Low	Flood	
Normal Above Normal	Flood	Mid	Slack	

Sampling Depth (meters):	Relative Depth:	Surface Bottom Midwater	Water Depth (meters):

Habitat Description and site comments:

Estimated Canopy Cover

Sampling activity comments:		Calibration check		
		Standard	Before Field	After Field
Temperature (C)	pH			
pH				
Conductivity (µs/cm)	Conductivity			
Salinity (ppt)	DO			
Dissolved Oxygen (mg/l)	Turbidity			
Dissolved Oxygen (%)				
Turbidity (NTU)			Entered into database? Check when yes -->	

Water Sample Container Labels:

Appendix F. Water Quality Research Within and Adjacent to Pacific Island Network Park Boundaries

Abbreviations

Parameters
T: Temperature
DO: Dissolved Oxygen
PAR: Photosynthetically Active Radiation
TN: Total Nitrate measured as NO_3
TP: Total Phosphate measured as PO_4
Chla: Chlorophyll a
Sal/cond: Salinity/conductivity

Agency
NPS: National Park Service
GEPA: Guam Environmental Protection Agency
DEQ: Commonwealth of the Northern Marianas Department of Environmental Quality
ASEPA: American Samoa Environmental Protection Agency
WWF: World Wildlife Fund
DOH: Hawaii Department of Health
EPA: United States Environmental Protection Agency
USGS: United States Geological Survey
NELHA: Natural Energy Lab of Hawaii
WAPPA: Waikaloa Anchialine Pond Preservation Area

Table F1. Timeline of water quality projects that included monitoring the core water quality parameters identified in this protocol within or immediately adjacent to park boundaries.

PARK	parameter	agency	program/project
WAPA	T	GEPA	CoastalEMAP
	T	NPS	reef sed 04-05
	T	GEPA	Beaches 90-00
	T	GEPA	Rivers1974-91
	pH	GEPA	CoastalEMAP
	pH	GEPA	Beaches
	pH	GEPA	Rivers
	sal/cond	GEPA	CoastalEMAP
	sal/cond	GEPA	Beaches
	sal/cond	GEPA	Rivers
	DO	GEPA	CoastalEMAP
	DO	GEPA	Beaches
	DO	GEPA	Rivers
	PAR	NPS	reef sed 04-05
	Turbidity	GEPA	CoastalEMAP
	Turbidity	GEPA	Beaches
	Turbidity	GEPA	Rivers
	TN	GEPA	CoastalEMAP
	TN	GEPA	Beaches
	TN	GEPA	Rivers
	TP	GEPA	CoastalEMAP
	TP	GEPA	Beaches
	TP	GEPA	Rivers
	depth/stage	USGS	Asan River in the Asan Unit (gage #16807600)
	depth/stage	USGS	Namo River at Santa Rita (gage #16808120) in the Agat Unit
AMME	T	DEQ	Beaches 1994 - 2005
	pH	DEQ	Beaches
	sal/cond	DEQ	Beaches
	sal/cond	NPS	Wetland 1990
	DO	DEQ	Beaches
	Turbidity	DEQ	Beaches
	TN	DEQ	Beaches
	TP	DEQ	Beaches
	chl a		
NPSA	T	ASEPA	EMAP 2004

Year columns (decades): 1970s, 1980s, 1990s, 2000s (each divided into years 0–9, and 0–5 for the 2000s).

Table F1. Timeline of water quality projects that included monitoring the core water quality parameters identified in this protocol within or immediately adjacent to park boundaries (continued).

PARK	parameter	agency	program/project	1970s 0	1	2	3	4	5	6	7	8	9	1980s 0	1	2	3	4	5	6	7	8	9	1990s 0	1	2	3	4	5	6	7	8	9	2000s 0	1	2	3	4	5
NPSA	T	NPS	1999 - 2005																																	▓	▓	▓	▓	▓	▓
	T	ACE	1980											▓																							▓				
	T	ASEPA	baseline 2001																																	▓				
	T	ASEPA	stream assessment 2003-2005																																			▓	▓	▓
	pH	ASEPA	EMAP																																			▓		
	pH	ASEPA	baseline 2001																																	▓				
	sal/cond	ASEPA	EMAP																																			▓		
	sal/cond	ACE	1980											▓																							▓				
	sal/cond	ASEPA	baseline 2001																																	▓				
	DO	ASEPA	EMAP																																			▓		
	PAR	ASEPA	EMAP																																			▓		
	Turbidity	ASEPA	EMAP																																			▓		
	TN	ASEPA	EMAP																																			▓		
	TP	ASEPA	EMAP																																			▓		
	chl a	WWF	Climate change 2002 - 2004																																		▓	▓	▓	
	chl a	ASEPA	EMAP																																			▓		
	depth	ASEPA	EMAP																																			▓		
USAR*	T	NPS	CRC 2002 - 2004																																		▓	▓	▓	
	T	USGS	Halawa stream 1983 to 1999														▓																							
	T	EPA	Coastal EMAP 2002/5																																		▓	▓	▓	▓
	T	DOH	Halawa Stream																																			▓	▓	▓
	pH	NPS	CRC 2002 - 2004																																		▓	▓	▓	
	pH	EPA	Coastal EMAP 2002/5																																		▓	▓	▓	▓
	pH	DOH	Halawa Stream																																			▓	▓	▓
	sal/cond	NPS	CRC 2002 - 2004																																		▓	▓	▓	
	sal/cond	EPA	Coastal EMAP 2002/5																																		▓	▓	▓	▓
	sal/cond	DOH	Halawa Stream																																			▓	▓	▓
	DO	NPS	CRC 2002 - 2004																																		▓	▓	▓	
	DO	EPA	Coastal EMAP 2002/5																																		▓	▓	▓	▓
	DO	DOH	Halawa Stream																																			▓	▓	▓
	Turbidity	EPA	Coastal EMAP 2002/5																																		▓	▓	▓	▓
	Turbidity	DOH	Halawa Stream																																			▓	▓	▓
	TN	EPA	Coastal EMAP 2002/5																																		▓	▓	▓	▓
	TN	DOH	Halawa Stream																																			▓	▓	▓
	TP	EPA	Coastal EMAP 2002/5																																		▓	▓	▓	▓

Table F1. Timeline of water quality projects that included monitoring the core water quality parameters identified in this protocol within or immediately adjacent to park boundaries (continued).

PARK	parameter	agency	program/project	70	71	72	73	74	75	76	77	78	79	80	81	82	83	84	85	86	87	88	89	90	91	92	93	94	95	96	97	98	99	00	01	02	03	04	05
USAR*	TP	DOH	Halawa Stream																															X	X				X
	chl a	EPA	Coastal EMAP 2002/5																																	X			X
	depth	NPS	CRC 2002 - 2004																																	X	X	X	
	depth	EPA	Coastal EMAP 2002/5																																	X			X
KALA	T	WCC	Limnology class																												X								
	T	NPS	Anchialine pools 2005																																				X
	T	USGS	Waikolu Stream (gages #16408000 and #16405500) 1969 to 1976	X	X	X	X	X	X	X							X																						
	T	USGS	Tunnel east portal (gage #16405100) 1975 to 1989						X								X																						
	pH	NPS	Anchialine pools 2005																																				X
	sal/cond	NPS	Anchialine pools 2005																																				X
	DO	NPS	Anchialine pools 2005																																				X
HALE	T	DOH	Beaches																									X											
	T	USGS	G#16501200 1972-83			X	X	X	X	X	X	X	X	X	X	X	X																						
	pH	DOH	Beaches																								X												
	pH	USGS	G#16501200 1972-83			X	X	X	X	X	X	X	X	X	X	X	X																						
	sal/cond	DOH	Beaches																																				
	sal/cond	USGS	G#16501200 1972-83			X	X	X	X	X	X	X	X	X	X	X	X																						
	DO	DOH	Beaches																																				
	Turbidity	DOH	Beaches																																				
	Turbidity	USGS	G#16501200 1972-77			X	X	X	X	X	X																												
	depth	USGS	G#16501200 1972-05			X	X	X	X	X	X	X	X	X	X	X	X	X	X	X	X	X	X	X	X	X	X	X	X	X	X	X	X	X	X	X	X	X	X
ALKA	T	DOH	Beaches 1973- 2005				X	X	X	X	X	X	X	X	X	X	X	X	X	X	X	X	X	X	X	X	X	X	X	X	X	X	X	X	X	X	X	X	X
	T	NELHA	CEMP 1983 - 2005														X	X	X	X	X	X	X	X	X	X	X	X	X	X	X	X	X	X	X	X	X	X	X
	T	NPS	Anchialine pools 2005																																				X
	T	EPA	Coastal EMAP 2002/5																																	X			X
	T	WAPPA	Waikoloa Anchialine Pond Preservation Area																																				
	pH	DOH	Beaches																																				
	pH	NELHA	CEMP 1983 - 2005														X	X	X	X	X	X	X	X	X	X	X	X	X	X	X	X	X	X	X	X	X	X	X
	pH	EPA	Coastal EMAP 2002/5																																	X			X
	pH	NPS	Anchialine pools 2005																																				X
	sal/cond	DOH	Beaches																																				
	sal/cond	EPA	Coastal EMAP 2002/5																																	X			X
	sal/cond	NELHA	CEMP 1983 - 2005														X	X	X	X	X	X	X	X	X	X	X	X	X	X	X	X	X	X	X	X	X	X	X
	sal/cond	NPS	Anchialine pools 2005																																				X
	sal/cond	WAPPA	Waikoloa Anchialine Pond Preservation Area																																				

Table F1. Timeline of water quality projects that included monitoring the core water quality parameters identified in this protocol within or immediately adjacent to park boundaries (continued).

PARK	parameter	agency	program/project
ALKA	DO	DOH	Beaches
	DO	EPA	Coastal EMAP 2002/5
	DO	NELHA	CEMP 1983 - 2005
	DO	NPS	Anchialine pools 2005
	DO	WAPPA	Waikoloa Anchialine Pond Preservation Area
	Turbidity	DOH	Beaches
	Turbidity	EPA	Coastal EMAP 2002/5
	Turbidity	NELHA	CEMP 1983 - 2005
	TN	DOH	Beaches
	TN	EPA	Coastal EMAP 2002/5
	TN	NELHA	CEMP 1983 - 2005
	TN	WAPPA	Waikoloa Anchialine Pond Preservation Area
	TP	DOH	Beaches
	TP	EPA	Coastal EMAP 2002/5
	TP	NELHA	CEMP 1983 - 2005
	TP	WAPPA	Waikoloa Anchialine Pond Preservation Area
	chl a	DOH	Beaches
	chl a	EPA	Coastal EMAP 2002/5
	chl a	NELHA	CEMP 1983 - 2005
	chl a	WAPPA	Waikoloa Anchialine Pond Preservation Area
	depth	EPA	Coastal EMAP 2002/5
	depth	DOH	Beaches
PUHE	T	DOH	Pelekane Bay Shoreline
	T	NPS	Anchialine pools 2005
	pH	DOH	Pelekane Bay Shoreline
	pH	NPS	Anchialine pools 2005
	sal/cond	NPS	Anchialine pools 2005
	sal/cond	DOH	Pelekane Bay Shoreline
	DO	DOH	Pelekane Bay Shoreline
	DO	NPS	Anchialine pools 2005
	Turbidity	DOH	Pelekane Bay Shoreline
	Turbidity	MKSWCD	Makeahua Gulch
	TN	DOH	Pelekane Bay Shoreline
	TP	DOH	Pelekane Bay Shoreline
			Anchialine pools/1999Chai

Timeline columns span: 1970s (0–9), 1980s (0–9), 1990s (0–9), 2000s (0–5).

Table F1. Timeline of water quality projects that included monitoring the core water quality parameters identified in this protocol within or immediately adjacent to park boundaries (continued).

PARK	parameter	agency	program/project
WAPA	T	GEPA	CoastalEMAP
	T	NPS	reef sed 04-05
	T	GEPA	Beaches 90-00
	T	GEPA	Rivers1974-91
	pH	GEPA	CoastalEMAP
	pH	GEPA	Beaches
	pH	GEPA	Rivers
	sal/cond	GEPA	CoastalEMAP
	sal/cond	GEPA	Beaches
	sal/cond	GEPA	Rivers
	DO	GEPA	CoastalEMAP
	DO	GEPA	Beaches
	DO	GEPA	Rivers
	PAR	NPS	reef sed 04-05
	Turbidity	GEPA	CoastalEMAP
	Turbidity	GEPA	Beaches
	Turbidity	GEPA	Rivers
	TN	GEPA	CoastalEMAP
	TN	GEPA	Beaches
	TN	GEPA	Rivers
	TP	GEPA	CoastalEMAP
	TP	GEPA	Beaches
	TP	GEPA	Rivers
	depth/stage	USGS	Asan River in the Asan Unit (gage #16807600)
	depth/stage	USGS	Namo River at Santa Rita (gage #16808120) in the Agat Unit
AMME	T	DEQ	Beaches 1994 - 2005
	pH	DEQ	Beaches
	sal/cond	DEQ	Beaches
	sal/cond	NPS	Wetland 1990
	DO	DEQ	Beaches
	Turbidity	DEQ	Beaches
	TN	DEQ	Beaches
	TP	DEQ	Beaches
	chl a		
NPSA	T	ASEPA	EMAP 2004

Timeline columns span decades: 1970s, 1980s, 1990s, 2000s (years 0–9, with 2000s shown 0–5).

Table F1. Timeline of water quality projects that included monitoring the core water quality parameters identified in this protocol within or immediately adjacent to park boundaries (continued).

PARK	parameter	agency	program/project
KAHO	depth	DOH	Honokohau Bay 1985-86
	depth	NPS	Anchialine pools/Maciolek &Brock 1974
	depth	NPS	Fishponds/199?Chai
PUHO	T	DOH	Beach 1973-1998 Honaunau Bay (City of Refuge)
	T	NPS	Anchialine pools 2005
	T	NPS	Anchialine pools/199?Chai
	T	NPS	Anchialine pools/2004Nakamura
	pH	NPS	Anchialine pools 2005
	pH	NPS	Anchialine pools/199?Chai
	pH	DOH	Beach 1973-1998 Honaunau Bay (City of Refuge)
	sal/cond	NPS	Anchialine pools 2005
	sal/cond	NPS	Anchialine pools/199?Chai
	sal/cond	NPS	Anchialine pools/2004Nakamura
	sal/cond	DOH	Beach 1973-1998 Honaunau Bay (City of Refuge)
	DO	NPS	Anchialine pools 2005
	DO	NPS	Anchialine pools/199?Chai
	DO	DOH	Beach 1973-1998 Honaunau Bay (City of Refuge)
	Turbidity	DOH	Beach 1973-1998 Honaunau Bay (City of Refuge)
	TN	DOH	Beach 1973-1998 Honaunau Bay (City of Refuge)
	TP	DOH	Beach 1973-1998 Honaunau Bay (City of Refuge)
	chl a		Anchialine pools/199?Chai
	depth		Anchialine pools/199?Chai
HAVO	T	NPS	Anchialine pools 2005
	pH	NPS	Anchialine pools 2005
	sal/cond	NPS	Anchialine pools 2005
	DO	NPS	Anchialine pools 2005
		NPS	Anchialine pools/199?Chai

Decade column headers: 1970s (0–9), 1980s (0–9), 1990s (0–9), 2000s (0–5)

*The scope of this table does not include monitoring data available for Pearl Harbor, the East Loch, and it's tributaries as they are not considered park waters The US Navy, USGS, UH Manoa, Leeward CC, and State of DOH have water quality data for these resources

Appendix G. GPRA Goals Addressed by the PACN Water Quality Protocol

Table G1. PACN park GPRA goals, relating to water quality and the assistance that the water quality protocol will give the parks in achieving goals

Park	GPRA Goals	Water Quality Protocol Assistance
AMME	No GPRA goals specifically relating to water quality.	While no specific assistance to the GPRA goals are addressed by the PACN water quality protocol, the strategic plan indicates that the wetlands are an "Area of Particular Concern" by the CNMI government because it is known habitat of endangered species. Water quality monitoring will aid the park in making management decisions relating to maintaining and determining any declines in the environmental integrity associated with a healthy wetland ecosystem in support of these endangered species.
WAPA	NPS Goal ID Number IIa1A: Percent of park visitors satisfied with appropriate park facilities, services, and recreational opportunities.	There are 1,002 marine acres within the park containing significant marine resources including coral reefs that are threatened by erosion and sedimentation carried by streams and rivers into the park. Degradation of the coral reef ecosystems within the park may contribute significantly to the decline in the quality and availability of diving and snorkeling opportunities available within the park, in addition to decreasing the biotic diversity and integrity of the park aquatic resources. Water quality monitoring will aid the park in assessing the status and trends of physical stressors present in the reef ecosystem and address the total load imported to these marine systems from the stream run-off.
NPSA	NPS Goal ID Number Ia2A: Populations of Federally listed species making progress toward recovery.	There are 2,550 marine acres within the park containing significant marine resources including coral reefs and the federally listed green sea turtles, hawksbill sea turtles, and humpback whales. Water quality can be of primary concern for threatened and endangered species, as degradation may lead to decreases in food quality and availability as well as decreasing effective foraging and refuge habitat. In addition, degradation of the water quality within the park may contribute to decreasing the biotic diversity and integrity of park aquatic resources, including coral reef ecosystems and freshwater streams. Water quality monitoring will aid the park in assessing the status and trends of the severity of physical stressors present in the reef and stream ecosystem.
USAR	No GPRA goals specifically relating to water quality.	While no specific assistance to the GPRA goals are addressed by the PACN water quality protocol, monitoring water quality within USAR may help to address physical parameters that may be useful in assessing the impact of changing water quality over time to the hull and hull faunal colonizers of the USS Arizona.

Table G1. PACN park GPRA goals, relating to water quality and the assistance that the water quality protocol will give the parks in achieving goals (continued).

Park	GPRA Goals	Water Quality Protocol Assistance
KALA	NPS Goal ID Number Ia1D: NPS managed riparian (stream/shoreline) miles in desired condition. NPS Goal ID Number Ia2A: Populations of federally listed species making progress towards recovery. NPS Goal ID Number Ia2B: Number of populations of species of management concern managed to desired condition. NPS Goal ID Number Ia4A: Miles of streams and rivers meeting state water quality standards. NPS Goal ID Number Ia4B: Acres of lakes, reservoirs, etc. meeting state water quality standards.	Monitoring the quality of water resources in KALA will help identify water quality conditions associated with the park's riparian systems that will aid in management decisions to achieve or maintain the desired conditions (Ia1D). KALA provides habitat and refuge for several marine and freshwater federally listed species. The water quality protocol will provide valuable information in assessing habitat conditions for all aquatic (marine, brackish, and freshwater) fauna, including federally listed species, to aid the park in management decisions associated with species recovery and managing populations to desired conditions (Ia2A and Ia2B). The water quality protocol will aid the park in monitoring water quality in nearshore coastal, brackish, and freshwater resources for temperature, pH, salinity, conductivity, turbidity, dissolved oxygen, total phosphorus, total nitrogen, and nitrate to assess coastal and watershed conditions and determine if state standards are being met (Ia4A and Ia4B).
HALE	NPS Goal ID Number Ia2A: Populations of federally listed species making progress towards recovery. NPS Goal ID Number Ia2B: Number of populations of species of management concern managed to desired condition. NPS Goal ID Number Ia4A: Miles of streams and rivers meeting state water quality standards.	HALE provides habitat and refuge for several freshwater federally listed species. The water quality protocol will provide valuable information in assessing habitat conditions for aquatic fauna, including federally listed species, to aid the park in management decisions associated with species recovery and managing populations to desired conditions (Ia2A and Ia2B). The water quality protocol will aid the park in monitoring water quality in nearshore coastal, brackish, and freshwater resources for temperature, pH, salinity, conductivity, turbidity, dissolved oxygen, total phosphorus, total nitrogen, and nitrate to assess coastal and watershed conditions and determine if state standards are being met (Ia4A and Ia4B).
PUHE	No GPRA goals specifically relating to water quality.	While no specific assistance to the park GPRA goals are addressed by the PACN water quality protocol, the water quality protocol will aid the park in monitoring water quality in brackish and freshwater resources for temperature, pH, salinity, conductivity, turbidity, dissolved oxygen, total phosphorus, total nitrogen, and nitrate to assess coastal and watershed conditions and determine if state standards are being met.

Table G1. PACN park GPRA goals, relating to water quality and the assistance that the water quality protocol will give the parks in achieving goals (continued).

Park	GPRA Goals	Water Quality Protocol Assistance
KAHO	NPS Goal ID Number Ia2A: Populations of federally listed species making progress towards recovery. NPS Goal ID Number IIa1A: Percent of park visitors satisfied with appropriate park facilities, services, and recreational opportunities. NPS Goal ID Number IaB: Number of archaeological sites in good condition.	KAHO provides habitat and refuge for hawksbill and green sea turtles, both federally listed species in addition to several species of coral. The water quality protocol will provide valuable information in assessing habitat conditions for marine fauna, including federally listed species, to aid the park in management decisions associated with species recovery and managing populations to desired conditions (Ia2A). Water quality monitoring will aid the park in assessing the status and trends of the severity of physical stressors present in the coral reef ecosystem. Degradation of the coral reef ecosystems within the park may contribute significantly to the quality and availability of diving and snorkeling opportunities available within the park, in addition to decreasing the biotic diversity and integrity of the park aquatic resources (IIa1A). KAHO also contains two historical fishponds of considerable size. Water quality monitoring within these fishponds will provide park management with information regarding the ongoing restoration processes in these fishponds (IaB).
PUHO	NPS Goal ID Number IaB: Number of archaeological sites in good condition.	PUHO contains fishponds that were associated with the ruling class of ancient Hawaii (ali'i). The park continues to maintain these fishponds both within and external to the refuge compound. Water quality assessments of these brackish fishponds will aid park management in making management decisions regarding the biotic integrity of these ponds.
HAVO	No GPRA goals related to water quality.	No specific GPRA goals are addressed by the water monitoring protocol; however, it may provide some interesting information regarding the alteration of physical parameters associated with the downstream effects in anchialine pools of the current and future eruptions from Kilauea.
ALKA	No GPRA goals -- Trail still under alignment process.	The water quality protocol will provide information relevant to ALKA only insomuch as it passes through the other parks on the west side of the Big island of Hawaii.

Appendix H. State, Territorial, and Commonwealth Water Quality Criteria

Table H1. State, Territorial, and Commonwealth water quality criteria.

Rule	Shall not vary from ambient conditions more than:			Allowable range:	Shall be greater than:
Parameter	Temperature as shown	Salinity (ppt)	pH	pH	Dissolved Oxygen as shown
Hawaii State WQS available at http://www.hawaii.gov/health/about/rules/11-54.pdf					
Fresh Streams	1.0 °C	n/a	0.5	5.5-8.0.	80 % saturation
Pearl Harbor	1.0 °C	10%	0.5	6.8-8.8.	60 % saturation
Marine coastal waters	1.0 °C	10%		7.6-8.6[2]	75 % saturation
GEPA WQS unavailable on-line; see Unified Watershed Assessment 1998 Clean Water Action Plan for Guam at http://www.guamepa.govguam.net/programs/water/GuamCWAP.pdf					
River Class S1	1.0 °C	n/a		6.5-8.5	5.6 mg/L
River Class S2	1.0 °C	n/a		6.5-8.5	5.6 mg/L
Marine Class M1	1.0 °C	10%	0.5	7.0-9.0	4.6 mg/L
Marine Class M2	1.0 °C	10%	0.5	7.0-9.0	4.6 mg/L
CNMI DEQ WQS available at http://www.deq.gov.mp/artdoc/Sec4art119ID277.pdf					
Fresh Surface Class 1	1.0 °C	n/a	0.5	6.5-8.5	75 % saturation
Marine Class A	1.0 °C	10%		7.5-8.6	75 % saturation
ASEPA WQS available at http://www.epa.gov/ost/standards/wqslibrary/territories/american_samoa_9_wqs.pdf					
Fresh Surface	1.5 °F[1]	none stated	0.2	6.5- 8.6	75% or 6.0 mg/L
Embayments	1.5 °F[1]	none stated	0.2	6.5- 8.6	70% or 5.0 mg/L
Open Coastal	1.5 °F[1]	none stated	0.2	6.5- 8.6	80% or 5.5 mg/L
Ocean	1.5 °F[1]	none stated	0.2	6.5- 8.6	80% or 5.5 mg/L

*Wet season: November 1 through April 30 for fresh water; and for open coastal waters receiving more than three million gallons per day of fresh water discharge per shoreline mile.

** Dry season: May 1 through October 31 for fresh water; and for open coastal waters receiving less than three million gallons per day of fresh water discharge per shoreline mile.

[1] Also, shall not fluctuate greater than 1°F hourly, nor exceed 85°F.

[2] Except at coastal locations where and when freshwater from stream, storm drain, or groundwater discharge may depress the pH to a minimum level of 7.0.

3) WQS specify chlorophyll *a* although the optical probe used in this protocol will be recording all forms of chlorophyll.

4) GEPA and DEQ criteria are for nitrate only (Hawaii State WQS use nitrate+nitrite) and do not specify whether value given is "as nitrogen."

5) TDS not greater than 500 mg/L or 133% from ambient, chlorine and sulfate not greater than 250 mg/L (if receiving saline discharges, no increase above 20% of ambient).

Table H1. State, Territorial, and Commonwealth Water Quality Standards.

Rule Parameter	Units	Conductivity	Chlorophyll a[1]	Turbidity	Shall not exceed: Total Phosphorous	Total Nitrogen	Nitrate + Nitrite Nitrogen[2]
		(micro-ohms/cm)	(ug/L)	(N.T.U.)	(ug P/L)	(ug N/L)	(ug [NO3+NO2]-N/L)
Hawaii State WQS Available At Http://Www.Hawaii.Gov/Health/About/Rules/11-54.Pdf							
Fresh Streams		300	none stated	5.0*/2.0**	50*/30**	250*/180**	70*/30**
Pearl Harbor		n/a	3.5	4.0	60	300	15
Marine Coastal Waters		n/a	0.3*/0.15**	50*/20**	20*/16**	150*/110**	5.0*/3.5**
GEPA WQS Unavailable On-Line; See Unified Watershed Assessment 1998 Clean Water Action Plan For Guam At Http://Www.Guamepa.Govguam.Net/Programs/Water/Guamcwap.Pdf							
River Class S1		n/a	none stated	0.5	none stated	none stated	0.10 mg/L
River Class S2		n/a	none stated	1.0	none stated	none stated	0.20 mg/L
Marine Class M1		n/a	none stated	0.5	none stated	none stated	0.10 mg/L
Marine Class M2		n/a	none stated	1.0	none stated	none stated	0.20 mg/L
CNMI DEQ WQS Available At Http://Www.Deq.Gov.Mp/Artdoc/Sec4art119ID277.Pdf							
Fresh Surface Class 1		n/a		0.5 above ambient	100	750	none stated
Marine Class A				1.0 above ambient	50	750	500
ASEPA WQS Available At Http://Www.Epa.Gov/Ost/Standards/Wqslibrary/Territories/American Samoa 9 Wqs.Pdf							
Fresh Surface		none stated		5.0	150	300	none stated
Embayments		none stated	0.5	0.35	20	150	none stated
Open Coastal		none stated	0.25	0.25	15	130	none stated
Ocean		none stated	0.18	0.20	11	115	none stated

*Wet season: November 1 through April 30 for fresh water; and for open coastal waters receiving more than three million gallons per day of fresh water discharge per shoreline mile.

** Dry season: May 1 through October 31 for fresh water; and for open coastal waters receiving less than three million gallons per day of fresh water discharge per shoreline mile.

[1]WQS specify chlorophyll a although the optical probe used in this protocol will be recording all forms of chlorophyll.

[2]GEPA and DEQ criteria are for nitrate only (Hawaii State WQS use nitrate+nitrite) and do not specify whether value given is "as nitrogen."

Appendix I. State, Territorial, and Commonwealth 303(d) Listed Waters

Table I.1 State, regional, and commonwealth 303(d) listed waters [l]

Park	Unique or Pristine Resources[a]	303d[b]	Groundwater[c]	Inland Waters Designation[d]	Marine Waters Designation[e]	Marine Bottom Ecosystem Designation[f]
WAPA	Wetlands	Agana Bay and the Northern Guam Lens Aquifer	NGL perimeter is G2[g]	S3	Asan and Agat are designated M2.	NA
AMME	Wetlands	Saipan Lagoon	Management zones are currently under development[h]	Class 1[i]	Class A and AA[j]	NA[j]
NPSA[k]	Coastal waters off Ofu and Tau, and Laufuti Stream	None	1G and 2G	Class 1 and Class 2	Embayment and Open Coastal	NA
USAR	None	Pearl Harbor	NA	NA	A	II
KALA	Kauhako crater lake and coastal waters	None	NA[c]	1a	AA	I
HALE	Streams, springs, sub-alpine lakes, and coastal Kipahulu district waters	None	NA[c]	1a (possibly 1b)	AA[j]	I[j]
ALKA	Park traverses coastal waters, wetlands, streams, and anchialine pool complexes	Pelekane Bay, Spencer Park Beach, Hapuna Beach, Kailua Bay, Magic Sands Beach, and Kealakekua Bay	NA[c]	1a	A and AA[j]	I and II[j]

Table I.1 State, regional, and commonwealth 303(d) listed waters (continued).

Park	Unique or Pristine Resources[a]	303d[b] Groundwater[c]	Inland Waters Designation[d]	Marine Waters Designation[e]		Marine Bottom Ecosystem Designation[f]
PUHE	None	Pelekane Bay	NA[c]	1a	AA	II
KAHO	Wetlands, anchialine pools, and coastal waters	None	NA[c]	1a	A and AA	I and II
PUHO	anchialine pools and coastal waters	None	NA[c]	1a	AA[j]	II[j]
HAVO	anchialine pools, coastal waters, and Olaa bogs	None	NA[c]	1a	AA[j]	II[j]

NA: Not applicable to this park.

[a] Outstanding Natural Resource Waters have not been designated in the PACN region.

[b] Refers to a section of the Clean Water Act that requires states to identify and list impaired water bodies (see http://www4.law.cornell.edu/uscode/33/1313.html for full details).

[c] Groundwater designations have not been developed by the State of Hawaii. For identification and description of Hawaiian Island aquifers see Mink, John F. and L. Stephen Lau. 1990–1993. "Aquifer Identification and Classification of Hawaiian Islands: Groundwater Protection Strategy for Hawaii" (6 reports) for the University of Hawaii Water Resources Research Center.

[d] See http://www.hawaii.gov/health/about/rules/11-54.pdf for full details.

[e] See http://www.hawaii.gov/health/about/rules/11-54.pdf for full details.

[f] see http://www.hawaii.gov/health/about/rules/11-54.pdf for full details.

[g] From the Unified Watershed Assessment 1998 Clean Water Action Plan for Guam available at http://www.guamepa.govguam.net/programs/water/Guam_CWAP.pdf

[h] See http://www.deq.gov.mp/artdoc/Sec9art52ID133.pdf for full details.

[i] See http://www.deq.gov.mp/artdoc/Sec9art52ID133.pdf for full details.

[j] Authorized park boundary only borders, does not encompass, marine waters.

[k] See http://www.epa.gov/ost/standards/wqslibrary/territories/american_samoa_9_wqs.pdf for full details.

Appendix J. Personnel Names and Contact Information

This appendix to the protocol narrative identifies past and current names and contact information of various personnel identified in Chapter 5. Titles of positions are based on those in Chapter 5. Current personnel are listed in Table J.1 As personnel change, new names will be added and individual tables added for each position as the example in Table J0.02.

Table Field Definitions

Name
Name of individual holding position. If no individual is assigned for a time period, designate as "Vacant". If a responsibility is delegated, such as the PACN Data Manager delegates the role to a subordinate, identify the individual to whom responsibility is delegated. The most recent/present individual with this responsibility is always listed first, followed in chronological order by predecessors.

Start Date
Initial date the named individual assumed this responsibility. Note, only a single, contiguous time period is referenced for each table row. If one individual assumes the same role for multiple non-contiguous time periods, each period of time shall be referenced in a separate table row.

End Date
Terminal date the named individual relinquished and was relieved (whew!!) of this responsibility.

Role
Formal or Acting: Boolean response indicating if this responsibility was assigned as part of standard job duties (formal), or assigned in a temporary capacity and temporary time period while other arrangements were being made (acting).

Physical Duty Station Address
Mailing address.

Park Administratively Assigned
Park or office where named individual is formally stationed.

Job Title
Official OPM type, including grade, if appropriate.

Email
Email address used.

Phone
Phone address used.

Table J1. Current individuals holding positions listed in Chapter 5 of Water Quality Vital Signs Monitoring Protocol for the Pacific Island Network report narrative.

	PACN Aquatic Ecologist	Park Lead	Aquatic Biological Technician	PACN Data Manager
Name	Tahzay Jones	Eric Brown	Lindsey Kramer	Kelly Kozar
Start Date	01 Jan 2007	01 Jan 2007	13 Aug 2007	1 Nov 2007
End Date	Present	Present	Present	Present
Role	Formal	Formal	Formal	Formal
Physical Duty Station Address	PO Box 52 Hawaii National Park, HI 96718	PO Box 2222, Kalaupapa, HI 96742	73-4786 Kanalani Street, #14 Kailua-Kona, HI 96740	PO Box 52, Hawaii National Park, HI 96718
Park Assigned	HAVO	KALA	KAHO	HAVO
Job Title	PACN Aquatic Ecologist	Marine Ecologist	Aquatic Biological Technician	PACN Data Manager
Email	tahzay_jones@nps.gov	eric_brown@nps.gov	lindsey_kramer@nps.gov	kelly_kozar@nps.gov
Phone	808-985-6188	808-567-6802 x40	808-329-6881 x318	808-985-6186

Table J.2 Historical record of individuals holding Project Lead position.

	Project Lead #1
Name	Tahzay Jones
Start Date	01 Jan 2006
End Date	Present
Role	Formal
Physical Duty Station Address	PO Box 52 Hawaii National Park, HI 96718
Park Assigned	HAVO
Job Title	PACN Aquatic Ecologist
Email	tahzay_jones@nps.gov
Phone	808-985-6188

Appendix K. Roles and Responsibilities

Role	Responsibilities	Name / Position
Project Lead	• Project oversight and administration • Track project objectives, budget, requirements, and progress toward project objectives • Facilitate communications between NPS and cooperator(s) • Coordinate and ratify changes to protocol • Assist in training field crews • Assist in performing data summaries and analysis, assist interpretation and report preparation • Review annual reports and other project deliverables for completeness and compliance with Inventory and Monitoring Program specifications • Maintain and archive project records • Upload certified data annually to NPSTORET • Project operations and implementation • Certify each season's data for quality and completeness • Complete reports, metadata, and other products according to schedule	Tahzay Jones, PACN Aquatic Ecologist
Data Analyst	• Perform data summaries and analysis, assist interpretation and report preparation	Tahzay Jones, PACN Aquatic Ecologist
Field Lead	• Train and ensure safety of field crew • Plan and execute field visits • Acquire and maintain field equipment • Oversee data collection and entry, verify accurate data transcription into database • Complete a field season report	Lindsey Kramer, Aquatic Biological Technician
Technicians	• Collect, record, enter and verify data	Anne Farahi, HAVO
Data Manager	• Consultant on data management activities • Facilitate check-in, review and posting of data, metadata, reports, and other products to national databases and clearinghouses according to schedule • Maintain and update database application • Provide database training as needed	Kelly Kozar , Data Manager, HAVO
GIS Specialist	• Consultant on spatial data collection, GPS use, and spatial analysis techniques • Facilitate spatial data development and map output generation • Work with Project Lead and Data Analyst to analyze spatial data and develop metadata for spatial data products • Primary steward of GIS data and products	Ben McMillan, GIS Technician, HAVO
Program Manager	• Review annual reports for completeness and compliance with I&M standards and expectations	Gregory Kudray
Park Biologists	• Facilitate logistics planning and coordination • Ensure project compliance with park requirements • Review reports, data and other project deliverables	Park Biologists and Resource Managers

Appendix L. Yearly Project Task List

Table L.1 This table identifies each task by project stage, indicates who is responsible, and establishes the timing for its execution. Protocol sections and SOPs are referred to as appropriate.

Project Stage	Task Description	Responsibility	Timing
Preparation	Initiate announcements for seasonal technician positions, begin hiring	Project Lead	Nov-Jan
	Notify Data Manager and GIS Specialist of needs for the coming season (field maps, GPS support, training)	Project Lead	by Dec 1
	Meet (or conference call) to recap past field season, discuss the upcoming field season, and document any needed changes to field sampling protocols or the working database	Project Lead, NPS Lead, Park Biologists, and Data Manager, GIS Specialist	Jan
	Ensure all project compliance needs are completed for the coming season	Park Biologists	Jan-Feb
	Provide names of field crew to Park Biologists	Project Lead	mid-Feb
	Plan schedule and logistics, including ordering any needed equipment and supplies (SOP #1)	Project Lead, NPS Lead, and Park Biologists	by Mar 1
	Inform GIS Specialist and Data Manager of specific needs for upcoming field season	Project Lead	by Mar 31
	Generate field navigation reports, roster of sample points and coordinates from the database (SOP #6)	Project Lead	by Mar 31
	Prepare and print field maps (SOP #6)	Project Lead	by Apr 15
	Update and load data dictionary, background maps, and target coordinates into GPS units (SOP #4)	GIS Specialist	by Apr 15
	Ensure that project workspace is ready for use and GPS download software is loaded at each park (SOP #10)	NPS Lead, Data Manager and GIS Specialist	by Apr 30
	Implement working database copy	Data Manager	by May 1
	Initiate computer access and key requests (may need park-specific dates)	Park Biologists	May
	Provide field crew email addresses and user logins to Data Manager	Park Biologists	May
	Provide database/GPS training as needed	Data Manager and GIS Specialist	May
	Train field crew in sampling protocols, and safety (SOP #2)	Field Lead	May
	Examination and certification of field observer qualifications, enter training results into database (SOP #2)	Field Lead	May

Project Stage	Task Description	Responsibility	Timing
Data Acquisition	Notify Park Biologist and Project Lead of tour itinerary	Technicians	Before each tour
	Collect field observations and position data during field trips	Technicians	May-Jul
	Review data forms after each day	Technicians	daily
	Check in with Park Biologist	Technicians	after each tour
	De-brief crew on operations, field methods, gear needs	Field Lead	after each tour
Data Entry & Processing	Download GPS data and email files to GIS Specialist for correction (SOP #4)	Technicians	after each tour
	Download and process digital images (SOP #12)	Technicians	after each tour
	Enter data into working copy of the database (SOP #13)	Technicians	after each tour
	Verification of accurate transcription as data are entered	Technicians	after each tour
	Upload working copy of the database to the networked server (I:\ drive)	Technicians	after each tour
	Correct GPS data and send screen capture to Field Lead and Project Lead for review	GIS Specialist	after each tour
	Periodic review of GPS location data and database entries for completeness and accuracy	Field Lead	bi-weekly
	Merge, correct, and export GPS data. Upload processed and verified coordinates to database	GIS Specialist	August
Product Development	Complete field season report	Field Lead	Jul-Aug
Product Delivery	Send field season report to NPS Lead, Park Biologists, Data Manager, and GIS Specialist	Project Lead	by Sep 30
Quality Review	Quality review and data validation using database tools (SOP #14)	Project Lead	Aug-Oct
	Prepare coordinate summaries and/or GIS layers and data sets as needed for spatial data review	GIS Specialist	by Sep 15
	Joint quality review of GIS data, determine best coordinates for subsequent mapping and field work	Project Lead and GIS Specialist	Sep-Oct
Metadata	Identify any sensitive information contained in the data set (SOP #16)	Project Lead and NPS Lead	Aug-Oct
	Update project metadata records (SOP #15)	Project Lead and NPS Lead	Aug-Oct
Data Certification & Delivery	Certify the season's data and complete the certification report (SOP #14)	Project Lead	Jan

72

Project Stage	Task Description	Responsibility	Timing
	Deliver certification report, certified data, digital photographs, and updated metadata to Data Manager (SOP #17)	NPS Lead	Jan
	Upload certified data into master project database, store data files in PACN Digital Library [1] (SOP #18)	Data Manager	Jan
	Notify Project Lead of uploaded data ready for upload to NPSTORET, analysis, and reporting.	Data Manager	Jan
	Update project GIS data sets, layers and associated metadata records	GIS Specialist	Dec-Jan
	Finalize and parse metadata records, store in PACN Digital Library [1] (SOP #15)	Data Manager and GIS Specialist	by Mar 15
Data Analysis	Examine data for spatial and temporal status and trends (SOP#19)	Data Analyst	Feb-Mar
Reporting & Product Development	Export automated summary queries and reports from database	Data Analyst	Feb-Mar
	Produce park-wide and transect-specific map output for archives	GIS Specialist	Mar
	Generate report-quality map output for reports	GIS Specialist	Mar
	Acquire the proper report template from the NPS website, create annual report	Project Lead	Mar
	Screen all reports and data products for sensitive information (SOP #19)	Project Lead and Park Biologist/Ecologists	Apr
	Prepare draft report and distribute to Park Biologists/Ecologists for preliminary review	Project Lead and NPS Lead	Apr
Product Delivery	Submit draft I&M report to Network Coordinator for review	Project Lead	May
	Review report for formatting and completeness, notify Project Lead of approval or need for changes	Program Manager	July
	Upload completed report to PACN Digital Library[1] submissions folder, notify Data Manager (SOP #17)	Project Lead or Data Manager	upon approval
	Deliver other products according to the delivery schedule and instructions (SOP #17)	Project and NPS Leads	upon completion
	Product check-in	Data Manager	upon receipt
Posting & Distribution	Submit data to NPStoret	Data Manager	by Mar 15
Archival & Records Management	Store finished products in PACN Digital Library [1]	Data Manager	upon receipt

Project Stage	Task Description	Responsibility	Timing
	Review, clean up and store and/or dispose of project files according to NPS Director's Order #19 [5]	NPS Lead and Project Lead	Jan
Season Close-out	Inventory equipment and supplies	Field Lead	Sept
	Conference call to discuss recent field season (close out); discuss who needs to do what to get data ready for analysis	Project Lead, NPS Lead, Park Biologists, Data Manager, and GIS specialist	by Oct 15
	Discuss and document needed changes to analysis and reporting procedures	Project Lead, NPS Lead, Park Biologists, and Data Manager	by Apr 30

[1]The PACN Digital Library is a hierarchical digital filing system stored on the PACN file server. Network users have read-only access to these files, except where information sensitivity may preclude general access.

[2]NPS Data Store is a clearinghouse for natural resource data and metadata. Only non-sensitive information is posted to NPS Data Store. Refer to the protocol section on sensitive information for details.

[3]NatureBib is the NPS bibliographic database (http://www.nature.nps.gov/nrbib/index.htm). This application has the capability of storing and providing public access to image data (e.g., PDF files) associated with each record.

[4]NPSpecies is the NPS database and application for maintaining park-specific species lists and observation data (http://science.nature.nps.gov/im/apps/npspp/).).

[5]NPS Director's Order 19 provides a schedule indicating the amount of time that the various kinds of records should be retained. Available at: http://data2.itc.nps.gov/npspolicy/DOrders.cfm

Appendix M. Database Documentation

The database for this project consists of four types of tables: core tables describing the "who, where and when" of data collection, project-specific tables, lookup tables that contain domain constraints for other tables, and cross reference tables that link lookup tables with data tables. Although core tables are based on PACN standards, they may contain fields, domains or descriptions that have been added or altered to meet project objectives.

The database includes the following standard tables:

tbl_Sites	Sample sites: individual parks
tbl_Locations	Sample locations: water quality sample stations
tbl_Events	Data collection event for a given location
tbl_Event_Details	Data collection event details such as environmental conditions.
tbl_Activity	Water quality activities performed during an event.
tbl_Event_Pics	Images of the sampling location for a particular event
tbl_Location_Pics	Images of the sampling location at the initial visit

The following are project-specific data tables:

tbl_Analytical_Procedures	User entered analytical procedures. Imported table structure from NPSTORET.
tbl_Field_Procedures	User entered field procedures. Imported table structure from NPSTORET.
tbl_Gear_Configurations	User entered gear configurations. Imported table structure from NPSTORET.
tb_Labs	User entered labs. Imported table structure from NPSTORET.
tbl_Lab_Sample_Prep	User entered lab sample preparation procedures. Imported table structure from NPSTORET.
tbl_PreserveTransportStore	User entered preservation, transport, and storage procedures. Imported table structure from NPSTORET.
tbl_Results	Water quality results

The following are a few of the more prominent, standard lookup tables:

tlu_ActivityTypes	List of Activity Types from WQX STORET including translation from Modern STORET
tlu_Addresses	Look up table of addresses. Linked to contacts in tlu_Contacts.
tlu_Characteristics	User entered characteristic definitions (parameters that are measured)
tlu_Contacts	Contacts related to the water quality protocol

The following are cross reference tables:

xref_Contact_Address	Cross-reference table between contacts and addresses
xref_Event_Contacts	Cross-reference table between events and contacts

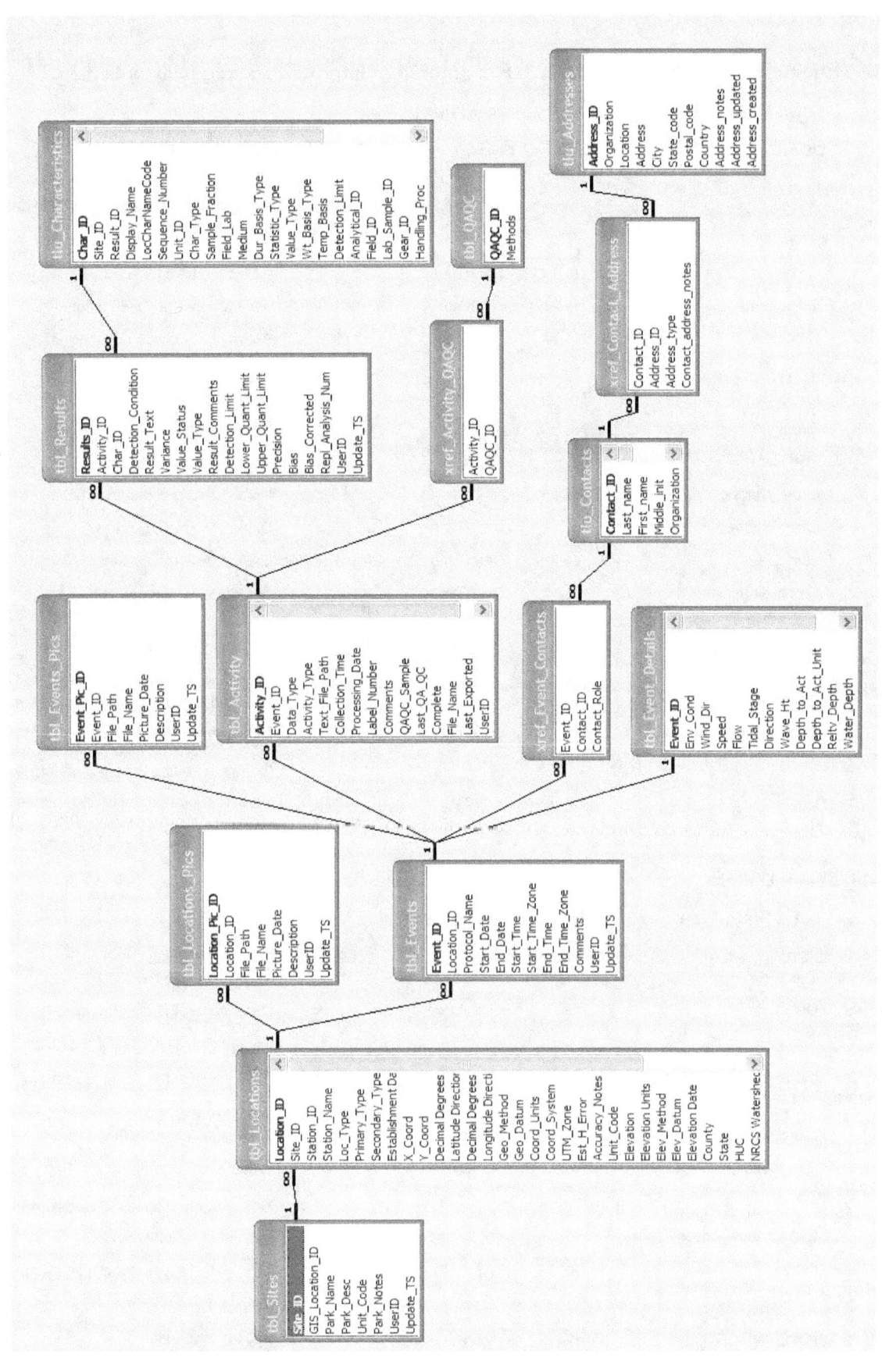

tbl_Activity   **User entered or imported water quality activities.**

Total Field Size: 698 **# Memo Fields:** 1

Field	Primary?	Field	Field Size	Field Description
Activity_ID	Yes	Other	16	Unique record identifier
Activity_Type	No	Long Integer	4	Activity type used for determining data entry form for results
Collection_Time	No	Date/Time	8	Collection time for activity
Comments	No	Memo	0	Activity comment/description
Complete	No	Boolean	1	Activity OK to write out after passing through QA checks
Data_Type	No	Text	50	Type of data collected, ie. YSI, Nutrient Data
Event_ID	No	Other	16	Record identifier for tbl_Events
File_Name	No	Text	255	Exported activity file name
Label_Number	No	Text	50	Water sample container label number
Last_Exported	No	Date/Time	8	Date activity last exported
Last_QA_QC	No	Date/Time	8	Date of last QA/QC check
Processing_Date	No	Date/Time	8	The date that the nutrient data was processed by the lab
QAQC_Sample	No	Text	3	Is this a QA/QC Sample?
Text_File_Path	No	Text	255	The file path for the text file that the data was imported from for the sampling event
Update_TS	No	Date/Time	8	Date/Time of last update - automatically stamp today's date/time in before update event
UserID	No	Text	8	Who last updated the record - automatically filled in by whoever logged on the system

tbl_Event_Details   **Sampling event details.**

Total Field Size: 96 **# Memo Fields:** 1

Field	Primary?	Field	Field Size	Field Description
Event_ID	Yes	Other	16	M. Event ID (Event_ID)
Depth_to_Act	No	Double	8	Distance/depth from surface to the point in water column at which the activity is conducted
Depth_to_Act_Unit	No	Text	2	Units in which the depth to activity is expressed (ft or m)
Direction	No	Text	5	Tidal direction; Ebb, Flood, Slack
Env_Cond	No	Text	14	Weather conditions; Sunny, Partly Sunny, Cloudy, Mostly Sunny, Cloudy, Overcast, Rain
Est_Canopy_Cover	No	Long Integer	4	Estimated canopy cover
Flow	No	Text	12	Flow level; Dry, No Flow, Low, Normal, Above Normal, Flood
Hab_Desc	No	Memo	0	Habitat description

Field	Primary?	Field	Field Size	Field Description
Reltv_Depth	No	Text	15	Approximate relative depth at which the
activity				occurred (Bottom, Midwater, Surface,
Subbottom,				
Speed	No	Long Integer	4	Wind speed in mph
Tidal_Stage	No	Text	4	Tidal stage; High, Low, Mid
Water_Depth	No	Long Integer	4	Water depth in meters
Wave_Ht	No	Long Integer	4	Wave height
Wind_Dir	No	Long Integer	4	Wind direction; 0(N), NE(45), E(90), SE(135),
S(180),				SW(225), W(270), NW(315)

tbl_Events — Sampling events.

Total Field Size: 188 **# Memo Fields:** 1

Field	Primary?	Field	Field Size	Field Description
Event_ID	Yes	Other	16	M. Event identifier (Event_ID)
Comments	No	Memo	0	Comments about sampling event.
End_Date	No	Date/Time	8	MA. Ending date for the event
End_Time	No	Date/Time	8	MA. Ending time for the event
End_Time_Zone	No	Text	4	End Time Zone for Visit (needed because a
Visit				could extend across Daylight
Savings/Standard				
Location_ID	No	Other	16	M. Link to tbl_Locations (Loc_ID)
Protocol_Name	No	Text	100	M. The name or code of the protocol
governing the				event (Protcl_Nam)
Start_Date	No	Date/Time	8	M. Starting date for the event (Start_Date)
Start_Time	No	Date/Time	8	MA. Starting time for the event (Start_Time)
Start_Time_Zone	No	Text	4	Start Time Zone for Visit
Update_TS	No	Date/Time	8	Date/Time of last update - automatically
stamp				today's date/time in before update event
UserID	No	Text	8	Who last updated the record - automatically
filled in				by whoever logged on the system

tbl_Events_Pics — User entered station visit picture links.

Total Field Size: 566 **# Memo Fields:** 1

Field	Primary?	Field	Field Size	Field Description
Event_Pic_ID	Yes	Other	16	Unique record identifier
Description	No	Memo	0	Description of the image
Event_ID	No	Other	16	Unique identifier for tbl_Events
File_Name	No	Text	255	File name of the linked image
File_Path	No	Text	255	File path of the linked image
Picture_Date	No	Date/Time	8	Date the image was taken
Update_TS	No	Date/Time	8	Date/Time of last update - automatically
stamp				today's date/time in before update event

	Field	Primary?	Field	Field Size	Field Description
	UserID	No	Text	8	Who last updated the record - automatically
filled in					by whoever logged on the system

tbl_Locations — Sampling unit locations.

Total Field Size: 1111 **# Memo Fields:** 2

	Field	Primary?	Field	Field Size	Field Description
	Location_ID	Yes	Other	16	M. Location identifier (Loc_ID)
	Accuracy_Notes	No	Text	255	MA. Positional accuracy notes (Acc_Notes)
	Coord_System	No	Text	50	M. Coordinate system (Coord_Syst)
	Coord_Units	No	Text	50	M. Coordinate distance units (Coord_Unit)
all	County	No	Text	50	Name of Station's primary County reported in capital letters
	Decimal Degrees Latitude	No	Double	8	Decimal Degrees Latitude
	Decimal Degrees Longitude	No	Double	8	Decimal Degrees Longitude
	Depth Units	No	Text	2	Depth units of measure (cm, m, mi, km, in, ft)
	Elev_Datum	No	Text	50	Elevational datum
	Elev_Method	No	Text	50	Elevational method
	Elevation	No	Double	8	Station's elevation (XXXXX.XXX)
	Elevation Date	No	Date/Time	8	Date elevation was determined
if	Elevation Units	No	Text	2	Elevation units of measure (ft or m). Required Elevation is given
(Est_H_Error)	Est_H_Error	No	Single	4	MA. Estimated horizontal accuracy
DD-	Establishment Date	No	Date/Time	8	Date on which Station was established (MM-YYYY)
	Geo_Datum	No	Text	50	M. Datum of mapping ellipsoid (Datum)
	Geo_Method	No	Text	50	Geospatial method
	HUC	No	Text	8	Station's 8-digit Hydrologic Unit Code
	Latitude Direction	No	Text	5	Latitude direction. Defaults to N
(Loc_Notes);	Loc_Notes	No	Memo	0	MA. General notes on the location Information specific to the station
freshwater,	Loc_Type	No	Text	25	MA. Station's primary classification; marine, anchialine, or groundwater
	Longitude Direction	No	Text	4	Longitude direction. Defaults to W
	NHD Reach ID	No	Text	14	NHD 14-digit Reach ID
	NRCS Watershed ID	No	Text	12	Valid NRCS Watershed ID for Station
Ocean, Gulf of Far	OceanName	No	Text	14	Ocean Name for Ocean Stations (Atlantic Pacific Ocean, Arctic Ocean, Caribbean Sea,
	OceanShoreRelation	No	Text	10	Ocean station's shore relation: Near Shore or Shore
	Primary_Type	No	Text	50	Station's primary classification

Secondary_Type	No	Text	30	Station's secondary type classification.
Required if				Primary Type = Canal, Facility, or Wetland
Site_ID	No	Other	16	MA. Link to tbl_Sites (Site_ID)
State	No	Text	2	Two-digit postal abbreviation of Station's
primary				State
Station_ID	No	Text	50	Unique station identifier
Station_Name	No	Text	100	M. Name of the station (Station_Name)
Travel Directions	No	Memo	0	Travel directions (by route, track, path,
waterway,				etc.) to reach the station
Unit_Code	No	Text	12	M. Park, Monument or Network code
(Unit_Code)				
Update_TS	No	Date/Time	8	Date/Time of last update - automatically
stamp				today's date/time in before update event
UserID	No	Text	8	Who last updated the record - automatically
filled in				by whoever logged on the system
UTM_Zone	No	Text	50	MA. UTM Zone (UTM_Zone)
Water Depth	No	Double	8	Typical Depth of Water at sampling location
X_Coord	No	Double	8	M. X coordinate (X_Coord)
Y_Coord	No	Double	8	M. Y coordinate (Y_Coord)

tbl_Locations_Pics — User entered station picture links.

Total Field Size: 608 **# Memo Fields:** 1

Field	*Primary?*	*Field*	*Field Size*	*Field Description*
Location_Pic_ID	Yes	Other	16	Unique record identifier
Description	No	Memo	0	Description of the image
File_Name	No	Text	255	File name of linked image
File_Path	No	Text	255	File path of linked image
Location_ID	No	Other	16	Unique identifier for tbl_Locations
Picture_Date	No	Date/Time	8	Date the image was taken
Update_TS	No	Date/Time	8	Date/Time of last update - automatically
stamp				today's date/time in before update event
UserID	No	Text	50	Who last updated the record - automatically
filled in				by whoever logged on the system

tbl_QAQC — No description

Total Field Size: 16 **# Memo Fields:** 1

Field	*Primary?*	*Field*	*Field Size*	*Field Description*
QAQC_ID	Yes	Other	16	Unique record identifier
Methods	No	Memo	0	Quality assurance and quality control
methods.				

tbl_Results — User entered or imported water quality monitoring results.

Total Field Size: 205 **# Memo Fields:** 2

Field	Primary?	Field	Field Size	Field Description
Results_ID	Yes	Other	16	Unique record identifier
Activity_ID	No	Other	16	Unique identifier for tbl_Activity
Bias	No	Text	12	A consistent deviation of measured values from the true value, caused by systematic errors in a procedure, as determined by applying identical procedures to a specimen of known properties.
Bias_Corrected	No	Text	1	A code (Y/N) indicating whether the confidence level has been corrected for Bias.
Char_ID	No	Other	16	Unique identifier for tbl_Characteristics
Detection_Condition	No	Text	23	Result Detection Condition from STORET (Detected and Quantified, *Non-detect, *Present, *Present >QL, *Present <QL, *Not Reported)
Detection_Limit	No	Double	8	Represents the least amount of the target substance which could be detected by the instrument/analytical process employed to determine the result. Above this value the target
Lower_Quant_Limit	No	Double	8	Represents the least amount of the target substance which could be quantified by the instrument/analytical process employed to determine the result. Values above the minimum and below the maximum quantitation limits are
Precision	No	Text	12	Estimate of the maximum poss ble error in the result. (e.g., Counting error in determining radiological beta particle counts.)
Repl_Analysis_Num	No	Double	8	Number of replicate analyses conducted to determine the result value.
Result_Comments	No	Memo	0	Result Comment or Description
Result_Text	No	Memo	0	Result Value
Update_TS	No	Date/Time	8	Date/Time of last update - automatically stamp today's date/time in before update event
Upper_Quant_Limit	No	Double	8	Represents the largest amount of the target substance which could be quantified by the instrument/analytical process employed to determine the result. Values > Min and < Max
UserID	No	Text	8	Who last updated the record - automatically filled in by whoever logged on the system
Value_Status	No	Text	1	Value Status (F=Final; P=Preliminary)
Value_Type	No	Text	10	Result Value Type (Actual, Estimated, Calculated)
Variance	No	Text	50	Variance for point samples

tbl_Sites   **Location aggregations.**

	Total Field Size:	415 **# Memo Fields:**	1		

Field	*Primary?*	*Field*	*Field Size*	*Field Description*
Site_ID	Yes	Other	16	M. Site identifier (Site_ID)
GIS_Location_ID	No	Other	16	MA. Link to GIS feature, equivalent to NPS_Location_ID (GIS_Loc_ID)
Park_Desc	No	Text	255	M. Description for a site (Site_Desc)
Park_Name (Site_Name)	No	Text	100	M. Unique name or code for a site
Park_Notes	No	Memo	0	MA. General notes on the site (Site_Notes)
Unit_Code (Unit_Code)	No	Text	12	M. Park, Monument or Network code
Update_TS stamp	No	Date/Time	8	Date/Time of last update - automatically today's date/time in before update event
UserID filled in	No	Text	8	Who last updated the record - automatically by whoever logged on the system

tblAnalyticalProcedures structure from

User entered analytical procedures. Imported table

NPSTORET.

	Total Field Size:	367 **# Memo Fields:**	1		

Field	*Primary?*	*Field*	*Field Size*	*Field Description*
Analytical_ID	Yes	Other	16	Analytical procedure unique identifier
Citation	No	Text	50	Analytical procedure citation
D_Last_update_TS stamp	No	Date/Time	8	Date/Time of Last Update - automatically today's date/time in before update event
D_UserID_code filled in	No	Text	8	Who last updated the record - automatically by whoever logged on the system
Description_text	No	Memo	0	Analytical procedure description text
Equip_Name the	No	Text	50	The name of the equipment being used for analytical procedure
Equip_Type analytical	No	Text	50	The type of equipment being used for the procedure
ID_Code	No	Text	15	Abbreviated name or identifying code for the analytical procedure - for NPSTORET
Name	No	Text	120	Full title of analytical procedure
National_Procedure	No	Text	50	Comparable national procedure

tblFieldProcedures from NPSTORET.

User entered field procedures. Imported table structure

	Total Field Size:	177 **# Memo Fields:**	1		

Field	*Primary?*	*Field*	*Field Size*	*Field Description*
Field_ID	Yes	Other	16	Unique field procedure identifier
Citation	No	Text	50	Field procedure citation
D_Last_update_TS stamp	No	Date/Time	8	Date/Time of last update - automatically

Field	Primary?	Field	Field Size	Field Description
				today's date/time in before update event
D_UserID_code	No	Text	8	Who last updated the record - automatically
filled in				by whoever logged on the system
Description_text	No	Memo	0	Descriptive text that provides more
information				about the field sampling procedure
Field_gear_type	No	Text	25	Category of field gear used (e.g. Water
Sampler,				Net/Vertical Tow, Benthic Dredge, Benthic
Corer,				
ID_Code	No	Text	10	Short name or code for field sampling
procedure -				for NPSTORET
Name	No	Text	60	Full name of the sampling procedure

tblGearConfigurations from

User entered gear configurations. Imported table structure from NPSTORET.

Total Field Size: 222 **# Memo Fields:** 1

Field	Primary?	Field	Field Size	Field Description
Gear_ID	Yes	Other	16	Gear configuration unique identifier
D_Last_update_TS	No	Date/Time	8	Date/Time of last update - automatically
stamp				today's date/time in before update event
D_UserID_code	No	Text	8	Who last updated the record - automatically
filled in				by whoever logged on the system
Description_Text	No	Memo	0	Specification/details about the tear
configuration				
Gear_Name	No	Text	50	The name of the gear for the configuration
Gear_Type	No	Text	50	The type of gear for the configuration
ID_Code	No	Text	10	Code identifying gear configuration within the organization - for NPSTORET
Model_Number	No	Text	50	The model number of the gear.
Name	No	Text	30	Name of the gear configuration

tblLabs NPSTORET.

User entered labs. Imported table structure from NPSTORET.

Total Field Size: 323 **# Memo Fields:** 0

Field	Primary?	Field	Field Size	Field Description
Lab_ID	Yes	Other	16	Laboratory unique identifier
Address_ID	No	Other	16	Link to tlu_Addresses
City	No	Text	50	City of the lab
Comments	No	Text	50	Any comments about the lab
D_Last_update_TS	No	Date/Time	8	Date/Time of last update - automatically
stamp				today's date/time in before update event
D_UserID_Code	No	Text	8	Who last updated the record - automatically
filled in				by whoever logged on the system
Electronic_address	No	Text	50	Email address of the lab

84

Field	Primary?	Field	Field Size	Field Description
ID_Code	No	Text	8	Lab ID Code - for NPSTORET
Name	No	Text	60	Lab Name
State	No	Text	2	State of the lab
Street_Address	No	Text	50	Street address of the lab
Zip_code	No	Text	5	Zip code of lab

tblLabSamplePrep table

User entered lab sample preparation procedures. Imported structure from NPSTORET.

Total Field Size: 167 **# Memo Fields:** 1

Field	Primary?	Field	Field Size	Field Description
Lab_Sample_ID identifier	Yes	Other	16	Lab sample preparation procedure unique
D_Last_update_TS stamp	No	Date/Time	8	Date/Time of Last Update - automatically today's date/time in before update event
D_UserID_code filled in	No	Text	8	Who last updated the record - automatically by whoever logged on the system
Description_Text description text	No	Memo	0	Lab sample preparation procedure
ID_Code lab	No	Text	15	Abbreviated name or identifying code for the sample preparation procedure - for NPSTORET
Name procedure	No	Text	120	Full title for the lab sample preparation

tblPreserveTransportStore procedures. Imported

User entered preservation, transport, and storage table structure from NPSTORET.

Total Field Size: 146 **# Memo Fields:** 1

Field	Primary?	Field	Field Size	Field Description
Preserve_ID identifier	Yes	Other	16	Preserve, transport, and storage unique
Container_color transport the	No	Text	10	Color of container used to collect and sample
Container_size_msr transport the	No	Single	4	Size of container used to collect and sample
Container_size_un	No	Text	3	Units of container size
Container_type_nm transport the	No	Text	32	Type of container used to collect and sample
D_Last_update_TS stamp	No	Date/Time	8	Date/Time of last update - automatically today's date/time in before update event
D_UserID_code filled in	No	Text	8	Who last updated the record - automatically by whoever logged on the system
ID_Code	No	Text	10	Short name or code for sample preservation, transport, and storage procedure - for NPSTORET

Name	No	Text	30	Full name of the sample preservation,
transport, and				storage procedure
Presrv_strge_prcdr	No	Memo	0	Chemical preservation and storage
procedure				description
Temp_presrv_type	No	Text	25	Name of the type of physical preservation

tlu_ActivityTypes   **list of Activity Types from WQX STORET including**
translation from

Modern STORET

Total Field Size: 403 **# Memo Fields:**   0

Field	Primary?	Field	Field Size	Field Description
ACTYP_UID	Yes	Long Integer	4	No description
ACTYP_CD	No	Text	70	No description
ACTYP_DESC	No	Text	255	No description
ModSTORETActivity	No	Text	70	No description
SortOrder	No	Long Integer	4	No description

tlu_Addresses **tlu_Contacts.**   Look up table of addresses. Linked to contacts in

Total Field Size: 382 **# Memo Fields:**   1

Field	Primary?	Field	Field Size	Field Description
Address_ID	Yes	Other	16	Unique record identifier
Address	No	Text	50	Street address
Address_created	No	Date/Time	8	Date the record was created
Address_notes	No	Memo	0	Any additional notes about the address
Address_updated	No	Date/Time	8	Date of last update to record
City	No	Text	50	City or town
Country	No	Text	50	Country
Location	No	Text	50	Location of organization
Organization	No	Text	50	Organization name
Postal_code	No	Text	50	Zip code (postal)
State_code	No	Text	50	State or Province

tlu_Characteristics measured)   User entered characteristic definitions (parameters that are

Total Field Size: 786 **# Memo Fields:**   1

Field	Primary?	Field	Field Size	Field Description
Char_ID	Yes	Other	16	Unique record identifier
Analytical_ID	No	Other	16	Link to analytical procedure
Char_Description	No	Memo	0	Describe or define more completely the characteristic definition
Char_Type characteristic	No	Text	50	What is the data type of the associated
Comp_Ind_CD defined entry	No	Text	1	Has the characteristic has been adequately (minimally required fields entered) for data
Det_Quant_Description	No	Text	255	Describe the meaning of the detection and/or quantification limits
Detection_Limit could be process that value, present.	No	Double	8	Least amount of the target substance that detected by the instrument or analytical was used to determine the result. Above this the target substance is presumed to be

Field Name	Required	Type	Size	Description
Display_Name	No	Text	60	Official EPA Characteristic Display Name
Dur_Basis_Type	No	Text	10	Time period over which a measurement was made
Field_ID	No	Other	16	Link to field sampling procedure
Field_Lab	No	Text	13	Where was the characteristic was measured
Gear_ID	No	Other	16	Link to gear configuration procedures
Handling_Proc	No	Other	16	Link to transport, preserve and storage procedures
Lab_Sample_ID	No	Other	16	Link to lab sample preparation procedure
LocCharNameCode	No	Text	60	Organization's Local Name for the Characteristic Definition
Lower_Quantity_Limit	No	Double	8	Lower Quantification Limit (often referred to as the Practical Quantitation Limit - PQL) represents the smallest amount of the target substance or characteristic that could be quantified by the instrument or analytical process.
Medium	No	Text	50	Medium in which the characteristic is measured
Result_ID	No	Other	16	Unique identifier for tbl_Results
Sample_Fraction	No	Text	50	No description
Sequence_Number	No	Single	4	Sequence number used for ordering characteristics on the results form. Characteristics are ordered in ascending order by sequence number.
ShowFilteredUnits	No	Boolean	1	Flag for whether to display all possible STORET units or filter the units based on the characteristic
Site_ID	No	Other	16	Unique identifier for tbl_Sites
Statistic_Type	No	Text	18	What type of statistic is the reported result value
Temp_Basis	No	Text	8	What is the controlled temperature at which the sample was maintained during analysis
Unit_ID	No	Other	16	Unit of Measure unique identifier
Update_TS	No	Date/Time	8	Date/Time of last update - automatically stamp today's date/time in before update event
Upper_Quantity_Limit	No	Double	8	Largest amount of the target substance that could be quantified by the instrument or analytical process. Values above the lower and below the upper quantification limits are reported as valid numeric results in STORET.
UserID	No	Text	8	Who last updated the record - automatically filled in by whoever logged on the system
Value_Type	No	Text	10	What type of value is the reported result

	Field	Primary?	Field	Field Size	Field Description
the	Wt_Basis_Type	No	Text	12	What is the form of the sample (or portion of
value					sample) that is associated with the result

tlu_Contacts — Look up table of contacts associated with the protocol.

Total Field Size: 659 **# Memo Fields:** 1

	Field	Primary?	Field	Field Size	Field Description
name,	Contact_ID	Yes	Text	50	Unique record identifier consisting of the last
					underscore, and first name of contact.
	Contact_created	No	Text	50	Date the contact record was created
protocol	Contact_is_active	No	Boolean	1	Is the contact currently associated with the
	Contact_location	No	Text	255	Contact's work locations
	Contact_notes	No	Memo	0	Notes about contact
	Contact_updated	No	Date/Time	8	Date the contact record was updated
	Email	No	Text	50	The email address of contact
	Fax	No	Text	25	Fax number
	First_name	No	Text	20	First name of contact
	Home_voice	No	Text	25	Home phone number
	Last_name	No	Text	24	Last name of contact
	Middle_init	No	Text	1	Middle initial of contact
	Mobile_voice	No	Text	25	Mobile phone number
with	Organization	No	Text	50	The organization the contact is associated
	Position_title	No	Text	50	Position title of contact
	Work_voice	No	Text	25	Work phone number

tlu_Geospatial (Methods and Datums) — Abbreviated geospatial table from STORET 10/10/2006

Total Field Size: 271 **# Memo Fields:** 0

	Field	Primary?	Field	Field Size	Field Description
	Category	No	Text	10	Geospatial category: Vertical or Horizontal
datum	Description	No	Text	255	Description of the Geospatial method or
	Subcategory	No	Text	6	Geospatial subcategory: Method or Datum

tlu_Permitted_Values — Non-STORET table containing permitted values for some of the STORET input fields in NPSTORET

Total Field Size: 102 **# Memo Fields:** 0

Field	Primary?	Field	Field Size	Field Description
Field_Name	No	Text	50	Name of the field for permitted values
Field_Value	No	Text	50	Permitted values for designated field
Sort_Order	No	Integer	2	Sort order

tlu_Primary_Type
NPSTORET

Look up table for water body types. Abbreviated version of table.

Total Field Size: 50 **# Memo Fields:** 0

Field	*Primary?*	*Field*	*Field Size*	*Field Description*
Primary_Type	No	Text	50	Water body type

tlu_Sample_Type
NPSTORET table.

Look up table for sample type. Abbreviated version of

Total Field Size: 54 **# Memo Fields:** 0

Field	Primary?	Field	Field Size	Field Description
Sample_Type	No	Text	50	Water quality sample type
Sort_Order	No	Long Integer	4	Sort order

tlu_Unit_of_Measure
(Units of

Look up table of units of measure from STORET 10/10/2006

Measure - Added and populated 'DISPLAY_NAME' field)

Total Field Size: 91 **# Memo Fields:** 0

Field	Primary?	Field	Field Size	Field Description
Description_Text	No	Text	50	Description of unit of measure
Display_Name	No	Text	10	Display name
Short_Form_Name	No	Text	10	Abbreviated unit of measure
Unit_ID	No	Other	16	Unique record identifier
UOM_Type	No	Text	5	Unit of measure type

tlu_Wind
Scale.

Look up table for the wind codes based on the Beaufort

Total Field Size: 108 **# Memo Fields:** 0

Field	Primary?	Field	Field Size	Field Description
Value	Yes	Double	8	Numeric value for wind speed
Description	No	Text	100	Definition of wind speed

xref_Activity_QAQC
assurance and

Cross-reference table between activities and quality

quality control.

Total Field Size: 32 **# Memo Fields:** 0

Field	Primary?	Field	Field Size	Field Description
Activity_ID	No	Other	16	M. Link to tbl_Activity
QAQC_ID	No	Other	16	M. Link to tbl_QAQC

xref_Contact_Address

Cross-reference table between contacts and addresses.

Total Field Size: 366 **# Memo Fields:** 0

Field	Primary?	Field	Field Size	Field Description
Address_ID	No	Other	16	M. Link to tlu_Address
Address_type	No	Text	50	Address type: physical address, mailing
address, or				mailing and physical address
Contact_address_notes	No	Text	250	Contact address notes
Contact_ID	No	Text	50	M. Link to tlu_Contacts

xref_Event_Contacts

Cross-reference table between events and contacts.

Total Field Size:	116 **# Memo Fields:**	0		

Field	*Primary?*	*Field*	*Field Size*	*Field Description*
Contact_ID	No	Text	50	M. Link to tlu_Contacts (Contact_ID)
Contact_Role (Cnt_Role)	No	Text	50	MA. The contact's role in the protocol
Event_ID	No	Other	16	M. Link to tbl_Events (Event_ID)

tbl_Append_Results text file in deleted after	Table that stores temporary data of imported results from a correct format for appending to appropriate tables. Data is each import.

Total Field Size:	186 **# Memo Fields:**	0		

Field	*Primary?*	*Field*	*Field Size*	*Field Description*
Activity_ID	No	Other	16	No description
Char_ID	No	Other	16	No description
Characteristic	No	Text	50	No description
Repl_Analysis_Num	No	Long Integer	4	No description
Result_Value	No	Text	50	No description
Variance	No	Text	50	No description

tbl_Avg_Results imported from a this table after	Table that stores temporary data of averaged results text file. Data is appended to tbl_Results and deleted from each import.

Total Field Size:	148 **# Memo Fields:**	0		

Field	*Primary?*	*Field*	*Field Size*	*Field Description*
Activity_ID	No	Other	16	No description
ChL	No	Double	8	No description
End_Date	No	Date/Time	8	No description
End_Time	No	Date/Time	8	No description
Event_ID	No	Other	16	No description
Location_ID	No	Other	16	No description
ODOSat	No	Double	8	No description
PAR	No	Double	8	No description
pH	No	Double	8	No description
Repl_Analysis_Number	No	Long Integer	4	No description
Sal	No	Double	8	No description
SpCond	No	Double	8	No description
Start_Date	No	Date/Time	8	No description
Start_Time	No	Date/Time	8	No description
Temp	No	Double	8	No description

Turbid+	No	Double	8	No description

tbl_Export_Results
import into

Table that temporarily stores result records formatted for
NPSTORET.

Total Field Size: 797 **# Memo Fields:** 4

Field	Primary?	Field	Field Size	Field Description
Activity_Comments	No	Memo	0	No description
Activity_Type	No	Long Integer	4	No description
Bias	No	Text	12	No description
Bias_Corrected	No	Text	1	No description
Contact	No	Text	255	No description
Detection_Limit	No	Double	8	No description
End_Date	No	Date/Time	8	No description
End_Time	No	Date/Time	8	No description
End_Time_Zone	No	Text	4	No description
Event_Comments	No	Memo	0	No description
Generated_Activity_ID	No	Text	255	No description
LocCharNameCode	No	Text	60	No description
Lower_Quant_Limit	No	Double	8	No description
Precision	No	Text	12	No description
QAQC_Sample	No	Text	3	No description
Repl_Analysis_Num	No	Double	8	No description
Result_Comments	No	Memo	0	No description
Result_Text	No	Memo	0	No description
Start_Date	No	Date/Time	8	No description
Start_Time	No	Date/Time	8	No description
Start_Time_Zone	No	Text	4	No description
Station_ID	No	Text	50	No description
Unit_Code	No	Text	12	No description
Upper_Quant_Limit	No	Double	8	No description
Value_Status	No	Text	1	No description
Value_Type	No	Text	10	No description
Variance	No	Text	50	No description

tbl_Export_Stations
import into

Table that temporarily stores station records formatted for
NPSTORET.

Total Field Size: 1398 **# Memo Fields:** 2

Field	Primary?	Field	Field Size	Field Description
Accuracy_Notes	No	Text	255	No description

95

Field	Primary?	Field Type	Field Size	Field Description
Coord_System	No	Text	50	No description
Coord_Units	No	Text	50	No description
County	No	Text	50	No description
Decimal Degrees Latitude	No	Double	8	No description
Decimal Degrees Longitude	No	Double	8	No description
Depth Units	No	Text	2	No description
Elev_Datum	No	Text	50	No description
Elev_Method	No	Text	50	No description
Elevation	No	Double	8	No description
Elevation Date	No	Date/Time	8	No description
Elevation Units	No	Text	2	No description
Est_H_Error	No	Single	4	No description
Establishment Date	No	Date/Time	8	No description
Geo_Datum	No	Text	50	No description
Geo_Method	No	Text	50	No description
GIS_Location_ID	No	Other	16	No description
HUC	No	Text	8	No description
Latitude Direction	No	Text	5	No description
Loc_Notes	No	Memo	0	No description
Loc_Type	No	Text	25	No description
Location_ID	No	Other	16	No description
Longitude Direction	No	Text	4	No description
Meta_MID	No	Other	16	No description
NHD Reach ID	No	Text	14	No description
NRCS Watershed ID	No	Text	12	No description
NRDTLocation_ID	No	Text	255	No description
OceanName	No	Text	14	No description
OceanShoreRelation	No	Text	10	No description
Primary_Type	No	Text	50	No description
Secondary_Type	No	Text	30	No description
Site_ID	No	Other	16	No description
State	No	Text	2	No description
Station_ID	No	Text	50	No description
Station_Name	No	Text	100	No description

tbl_Linked_Files
File linking
switchboard.

List of back-end data files used by the file linking utility.

accessed from the Tools button on the Dataset Catalog

Total Field Size: 306 **# Memo Fields:** 0

Field	*Primary?*	*Field*	*Field Size*	*Field Description*

LinkCategory	Yes	Text	50	Category of current link
LinkFile	No	Text	255	Path and file name of current link
SortOrder	No	Byte	1	Sort Order

tbl_Linked_Tables **List of tables in each of the back-end databases used by**
the file linking

Dataset Catalog **utility. File linking accessed from the Tools button on the**

switchboard.

Total Field Size: 100 **# Memo Fields:** 0

Field	*Primary?*	*Field*	*Field Size*	*Field Description*
LinkTableName	Yes	Text	50	Name of the linked table
LinkCategory	No	Text	50	Category of linked tables

qapp_Import_GPS **Appends data from the imported text file of GPS points to**
the table

tbl_Locations.

Query Type **Append**

Query SQL INSERT INTO tbl_Locations ([Decimal Degrees Latitude], [Decimal Degrees Longitude], Station_ID)
SELECT tblTXTImportTemp.lat, tblTXTImportTemp.long, tblTXTImportTemp.ident
FROM tblTXTImportTemp;

qapp_Import_Results **Appends imported result data from several different**
temporary tables

into tbl_Append_Results.

Query Type **Append**

Query SQL INSERT INTO tbl_Append_Results (Characteristic, Result_Value, Variance)
SELECT tbl_Trans_Results.Characteristic, tbl_Trans_Results.Result_Value, tbl_Trans_Variance.Variance
FROM tbl_Trans_Results INNER JOIN tbl_Trans_Variance ON tbl_Trans_Results.Characteristic =
tbl_Trans_Variance.Characteristic
WHERE (((tbl_Trans_Results.Characteristic)<>"Event_ID" And
(tbl_Trans_Results.Characteristic)<>"Activity_ID"));

qmak_Import_Results **Appends imported result data from several different**
temporary tables

into tbl_Append_Results.

Query Type **Make-table**

Query SQL SELECT tbl_Trans_Results.Characteristic, tbl_Trans_Results.Result_Value, tbl_Trans_Variance.Variance INTO
tbl_Alter_Results
FROM tbl_Trans_Results INNER JOIN tbl_Trans_Variance ON
tbl_Trans_Results.Characteristic=tbl_Trans_Variance.Characteristic

qry_Contact **Queries xref_Event_Contacts and tlu_Contacts for the first**
contact listed

for a sampling event in order to link to a sampling event in

qry_Export and

qry_Export_Format.

Query Type **Select**

Query SQL SELECT xref_Event_Contacts.Event_ID, First([First_Name] & " " & [Last_Name]) AS Contact
FROM tlu_Contacts INNER JOIN xref_Event_Contacts ON
tlu_Contacts.Contact_ID=xref_Event_Contacts.Contact_ID
GROUP BY xref_Event_Contacts.Event_ID;

qry_Event_Details **Queries data from tbl_Sites, tbl_Locations, tbl_Events, and tbl_Event_Details in order to format for import into NPSTORET.**

Query Type Select

Query SQL SELECT tbl_Sites.Unit_Code, tbl_Locations.Station_ID, tbl_Events.Start_Date, tbl_Events.End_Date, tbl_Events.Event_ID, tbl_Event_Details.Env_Cond, tbl_Event_Details.Wind_Dir, tbl_Event_Details.Speed, tbl_Event_Details.Flow, tbl_Event_Details.Direction, tbl_Event_Details.Wave_Ht, tbl_Event_Details.Water_Depth, tbl_Event_Details.Est_Canopy_Cover, tbl_Event_Details.Hab_Desc
FROM tbl_Sites INNER JOIN (tbl_Locations INNER JOIN (tbl_Events LEFT JOIN tbl_Event_Details ON tbl_Events.Event_ID=tbl_Event_Details.Event_ID) ON tbl_Locations.Location_ID=tbl_Events.Location_ID) ON tbl_Sites.Site_ID=tbl_Locations.Site_ID;

qry_Export **Queries data from tbl_Locations, tbl_Events, tbl_Activities, and tbl_Results in order to export data.**

Query Type Select

Query SQL SELECT tbl_Sites.Unit_Code, tbl_Locations.Station_ID, tbl_Events.Start_Date, tbl_Events.End_Date, tbl_Events.Start_Time, tbl_Events.Start_Time_Zone, tbl_Events.End_Time, tbl_Events.End_Time_Zone, qry_Contact.Contact, Left(tbl_Sites.Unit_Code,1) & Right(tbl_Sites.Unit_Code,1) & Right([Station_ID],1) & Left([Station_ID],1) & Right(DatePart("yyyy",tbl_Events.Start_Date),2) & DatePart("m",tbl_Events.Start_Date) & Minute(tbl_Activity.Collection_Time) & DatePart("d",tbl_Activity.Processing_Date) AS Generated_Activity_ID, tbl_Events.Comments AS Event_Comments, tbl_Activity.QAQC_Sample, tbl_Activity.Data_Type, tbl_Activity.Comments AS Activity_Comments, tlu_Characteristics.LocCharNameCode, tbl_Results.Detection_Condition, tbl_Results.Result_Text, tbl_Results.Variance, tbl_Results.Value_Status, tbl_Results.Value_Type, tbl_Results.Result_Comments, tbl_Results.Detection_Limit, tbl_Results.Lower_Quant_Limit, tbl_Results.Upper_Quant_Limit, tbl_Results.Precision, tbl_Results.Bias, tbl_Results.Bias_Corrected, tbl_Results.Repl_Analysis_Num
FROM tlu_Characteristics INNER JOIN (tbl_Sites INNER JOIN (tbl_Locations INNER JOIN ((tbl_Events LEFT JOIN qry_Contact ON tbl_Events.Event_ID = qry_Contact.Event_ID) INNER JOIN (tbl_Activity INNER JOIN tbl_Results ON tbl_Activity.Activity_ID = tbl_Results.Activity_ID) ON tbl_Events.Event_ID = tbl_Activity.Event_ID) ON tbl_Locations.Location_ID = tbl_Events.Location_ID) ON tbl_Sites.Site_ID = tbl_Locations.Site_ID) ON tlu_Characteristics.Char_ID = tbl_Results.Char_ID

qry_Export_Format **Queries data from tbl_Locations, tbl_Events, tbl_Activities, and tbl_Results in order to export data.**

Query Type Select

Query SQL SELECT tbl_Sites.Unit_Code, tbl_Locations.Station_ID, tbl_Events.Start_Date, tbl_Events.End_Date, tbl_Events.Start_Time, tbl_Events.Start_Time_Zone, tbl_Events.End_Time, tbl_Events.End_Time_Zone, qry_Contact.Contact, Left(tbl_Sites.Unit_Code,1) & Right(tbl_Sites.Unit_Code,1) & Right(tbl_Locations.Station_ID,1) & Left(tbl_Locations.Station_ID,1) & Right(DatePart("yyyy",tbl_Events.Start_Date),2) & DatePart("m",tbl_Events.Start_Date) & Minute(tbl_Activity.Collection_Time) & DatePart("d",tbl_Activity.Processing_Date) AS Generated_Activity_ID, tbl_Events.Comments AS Event_Comments, tbl_Activity.Activity_Type, tbl_Activity.QAQC_Sample, tbl_Activity.Comments AS Activity_Comments, tlu_Characteristics.LocCharNameCode, tbl_Temp_Results.Result_Text, tbl_Temp_Results.Variance, tbl_Temp_Results.Value_Status, tbl_Temp_Results.Value_Type, tbl_Temp_Results.Result_Comments, tbl_Temp_Results.Detection_Limit, tbl_Temp_Results.Lower_Quant_Limit, tbl_Temp_Results.Upper_Quant_Limit, tbl_Temp_Results.Precision, tbl_Temp_Results.Bias, tbl_Temp_Results.Bias_Corrected, tbl_Temp_Results.Repl_Analysis_Num
FROM tbl_Sites INNER JOIN (tbl_Locations INNER JOIN ((tbl_Events LEFT JOIN qry_Contact ON tbl_Events.Event_ID = qry_Contact.Event_ID) INNER JOIN ((tbl_Activity INNER JOIN tbl_Temp_Results ON tbl_Activity.Activity_ID = tbl_Temp_Results.Activity_ID) INNER JOIN tlu_Characteristics ON tbl_Temp_Results.Char_ID = tlu_Characteristics.Char_ID) ON tbl_Events.Event_ID = tbl_Activity.Event_ID) ON tbl_Locations.Location_ID = tbl_Events.Location_ID) ON tbl_Sites.Site_ID = tbl_Locations.Site_ID

qry_Results **Joins tbl_Results to tlu_Characteristics in order to display**

the results for

each characteristic in sfrm_Results.

Query Type **Select**

Query SQL SELECT tbl_Results.Results_ID, tbl_Results.Activity_ID, tbl_Results.Char_ID, tbl_Results.UserID, tlu_Characteristics.Sequence_Number, tbl_Results.Detection_Condition, tbl_Results.Result_Text, tbl_Results.Variance, tbl_Results.Value_Status, tbl_Results.Value_Type, tbl_Results.Result_Comments, tbl_Results.Detection_Limit, tbl_Results.Lower_Quant_Limit, tbl_Results.Upper_Quant_Limit, tbl_Results.Precision, tbl_Results.Bias, tbl_Results.Bias_Corrected, tbl_Results.Repl_Analysis_Num
FROM tlu_Characteristics INNER JOIN tbl_Results ON tlu_Characteristics.Char_ID=tbl_Results.Char_ID;

qry_Station_Check **Queries tbl_Locations to search for null values in fields that are required**

by NPSTORET.

Query Type **Select**

Query SQL SELECT tbl_Locations.Location_ID, tbl_Locations.Station_ID, tbl_Locations.Primary_Type, tbl_Locations.[Decimal Degrees Latitude], tbl_Locations.[Latitude Direction], tbl_Locations.[Decimal Degrees Longitude], tbl_Locations.[Longitude Direction], tbl_Locations.Geo_Method, tbl_Locations.Geo_Datum, tbl_Locations.County, tbl_Locations.State
FROM tbl_Locations
WHERE (((tbl_Locations.Station_ID) Is Null)) OR (((tbl_Locations.Primary_Type) Is Null)) OR (((tbl_Locations.[Decimal Degrees Latitude]) Is Null)) OR (((tbl_Locations.[Latitude Direction]) Is Null)) OR (((tbl_Locations.[Decimal Degrees Longitude]) Is Null)) OR (((tbl_Locations.[Longitude Direction]) Is Null)) OR (((tbl_Locations.Geo_Method) Is Null)) OR (((tbl_Locations.Geo_Datum) Is Null)) OR (((tbl_Locations.County) Is Null)) OR (((tbl_Locations.State) Is Null));

NPS 988/108133, June 2011